Expect Miracles

Expect Miracles

Dr. Joe Vitale

Published by BurmanBooks Inc.
260 Queens Quay West
Suite 904
Toronto, Ontario
Canada M5J 2N3

Cover and interior design: Jack Steiner Graphic Design
Editing: Kimberlee MacDonald

Distribution:
Trumedia Group
c/o Ingram Publisher Services
14 Ingram Blvd.
LaVergne, TN 37086

ISBN 978-1-89740406-5

Printed in Canada

Dedicated to the Divine

Acknowledgments

As with every book I've ever written, many people supported and encouraged me in the process. Nerissa, my life partner and love, is always there for me and always feeding the critters so that I can keep writing. I thank Rhonda Byrne, creator of the movie *The Secret*, for putting me in her amazing film so new people would hear of my work and want a book like this one. Suzanne Burns, my key assistant, makes my daily life easier so I can focus on writing. Close friends gave me support and advice. They include Bill Hibbler, Pat O'Bryan, Craig Perrine, Peter Wink and Cindy Cashman. My dear friend and fellow crusader of the light, Mark Ryan, is always supportive of my projects. Victoria Schaefer is totally supportive of me and my work and is a priceless friend. I thank Dee Burks for her writing and editing skills. I, of course, thank Sanjay Burman for his belief in me and for publishing this book. Finally, I'm grateful to the Divine for allowing me to do what I do. If I'm forgetting anyone and I probably am, I apologize. I love you all.

Table of Contents

Introduction

"All this, 'Don't worry, be happy' junk is total nonsense. You only tell people they can change their lives to make a buck. You're nothing but a salesman preying on innocent and delusional people."

While I don't hear comments like this one everyday, I do hear them. I don't live any sort of sheltered existence and I'm very aware of people who look on the whole field of self-development as total 'crapola.' One frequently asked question I get is, "If this stuff is real, then why doesn't it work for me?" The truth is, it does and it's working right now, but because you're still being held back by your own limiting beliefs, you feel that it isn't working. I know you may think this is some kind of circular logic designed to provide no real answers; it's anything but. The real answer is, it's you and it's always been you. You decide what you're worthy of, you decide how you choose to view life and you determine your own success or failure.

No matter how many seminars you attend or self help books you buy, you'll only go as far as your limiting beliefs will allow you to. Have you ever set a goal to lose 40 pounds, but only lost twenty? Have you ever tried to make $100,000 and only made $25,000? Have you ever wanted a BMW, yet still drive a Pinto? Your limiting beliefs tell your mind what is probable, rather than possible. The idea of expecting miracles is to open your life to unlimited possibility and reach those goals that may have eluded you so far.

This isn't to imply that it will be easy. I know what it's like to sleep in public restrooms because I had no where else to go. I know what it's like to owe money to everyone and their dog. I've sat in the front seat of the worst clunker car you can imagine and hoped against hope that it would start just one more time. If you'd asked me at the time if I was responsible for these situations, I would have probably said, "Absolutely not." After literally decades of wallowing in self pity, I realized that the problem was me; it was always me. Not only was I responsible for these situations, I had actually created them.

This may not have been what you expected to read on the first pages of a book called "Expect Miracles," but it's the truth. There are no techniques that will help you if you refuse to be helped. If you're not willing to look within yourself and get clear of your limiting beliefs, then you'll never know the abundance of miracles waiting to happen in your life.

There's no denying that miraculous events now happen to me every day. I attract them and expect them and they happen. I'm frequently asked by people how to attract miracles to their own lives and I can honestly say that you already experience miracles; we all do. That call from a long lost friend that you've been thinking about, the contractor you run into at the grocery store the day after your fence blows down or the refund from your doctor for overpayment of services are all minor miracles. Small events that appear in your lives almost daily are attracted by you, if you but choose to notice them. Many people push these little happenings aside or chalk them up to coincidence. Call it what you will, they still happen and if you choose to allow it, even bigger miracles can be attracted into your life.

My life has been and continues to be a wonderful adventure full of miracles that move me swiftly along the path to success and continual learning. Over the last few years, many of the concepts that I have written about in my books, such as *The Attractor Factor, Zero Limits* and *The Missing Key* have been used by many people with great success and they frequently email me their stories of miracles; many of which you will read in this book. But there are also occasionally emails from people who say they have tried my methods and nothing happened. They outline the intentions they set, the actions they took and even the events that then convinced them it wasn't working. They want to know why.

I decided to write this book because there is a key element that these people and many others are missing. It is common for people to say they want something; to be rich, to drive a hot sports car or they want to own the big house on the hill. However, locked within them are a whole slew of limiting beliefs that produce a constant stream of negative talk and may sound something like this:

"I don't deserve to be rich."

"Rich people are thieves."

"A hot car would get me killed."

"My wife will think I'm having a mid life crisis."

"If I buy a big house, everyone will want to borrow money from me."

"I'll feel guilty if I have a lot and others don't."

This negative self talk reveals the limiting beliefs that exist within your mind. Though you may say that you want to be rich, your limiting beliefs prevent you from attracting wealth. They become what I call counter intentions. Though you may say you have an intention to improve an area of your life, these counter intentions constantly pull you back from reaching your goal. Thus, you only lose 20 lbs. instead of 40, earn $25,000 instead of $100,000 and feel humiliated every time your Pinto backfires.

It's important to realize that there may be some counter intentions that are more persistent than others. This is especially true if you've tried some other personal development programs and been disappointed with the results; indicating that your beliefs are deep rooted and may take more time and work to overcome. But it can be done.

As you move through the steps presented in this book, you'll discover how to identify the limiting beliefs lurking in your mind and finally rid yourself of them. This opens the door to the miracles of wealth and abundance waiting to flow into your life.

I live in the beautiful hill country of Texas and one of my favorite activities is to relax in the hot tub outside in the evening and gaze up at the stars. Those are the same stars that witnessed my decline into homelessness decades ago, the same ones that watched me struggle and claw my way out of poverty and the same stars that saw my triumphs and fabulous success once I learned to expect miracles in my life. This truth exists as proof to me that the awesome spectacle of the universe doesn't change; it exists as it always has and is available for all who choose to partake of its bounty. I chose to change and my life has become and continues to become, more than I ever could have imagined or dreamed.

You may be skeptical, you may have been disappointed or you may be trying to rise to that next level of awareness and enlightenment. No matter the reason, you can choose to change and allow miracles into your life.

I challenge you to make the choice to get in the game and see where it leads, rather than sitting on the sidelines and throwing rocks at something you don't completely understand.

CHAPTER 1

Why Guru Advice Doesn't Work

Gurus offering advice on everything from weight loss to how to make millions are everywhere; radio, television, all over the bookstores. The movie, *The Secret*, has created a world wide growth and demand in those seeking their own personal path to a full and meaningful life. Most of these gurus are sincere and know what they're talking about because, like me, they've traveled the road themselves. It doesn't matter if it's Bob Proctor, Tony Robbins, Wayne Dyer, or Joe Vitale, we've all experienced our own trials in life and set out upon the path of improvement.

It's natural when you find the answers in your own life to want to share those answers with those around you. As I traveled my own path, I also committed myself to helping others travel theirs, as well. I frequently come across people who have tried a particular program or gone to a seminar and still haven't experienced success in their lives. They make statements like, "That kind of stuff doesn't really work; it's all hype," or "I fell for that once and bought all their stuff and it didn't make one bit of difference, so why should I believe you?" It's not uncommon for these people to view their own lack of results and then make a blanket statement that nothing will work for them. They frequently dismiss and discredit any other program, without even trying it.

I've also been told that none of this self-development stuff is anything new and that's absolutely correct. Most of this knowledge and wisdom has been around since ancient times. For centuries, people have sought to improve their lives and understand why we behave the way we do. Socrates is a great example of someone who sought the truth. The Socratic Method is rooted in the concept of breaking a problem down and asking numerous, probing questions to discern the truth and that's exactly what most self-development programs do. They require introspection; you have to ask yourself the hard questions. Why do you believe what you believe? Where did the beliefs come from? What are you willing to do to change your results? Socrates made it a point to approach people who were considered the wisest in Athens and ask them questions which forced them to examine their own ideas and beliefs. They hated it! They felt foolish and eventually found a way to get rid of him and have him sentenced to death.

Boy, am I glad they don't do that to self-development gurus today! The reason Socrates ended up in that situation is that the people he asked the questions didn't like what they saw within themselves. They liked the status quo they were living and became very angry when those beliefs were challenged. We do the same thing today. We'll try a program and say we want to be different, but when it comes to taking responsibility for the results in our lives, we feel bad and this can result in anger, sadness, and a reluctance to continue. It's easier to go back to what we've known than it is to struggle through unknown territory.

You'll notice that almost every self-development program has a slightly different take on what you need to do to achieve your goals. You might wonder why, if this knowledge has been around for centuries, someone hasn't figured out the one definite answer to life's problems? This is because different approaches work for different people. We haven't all had the same experiences and therefore don't have the same memories. Consequently, our perceptions and beliefs will all be slightly different and therefore we respond to different triggers.

For example, if you lose 80 pounds on program B, after having failed to lose any weight on program A, does that mean no one else can succeed on program A? No, it doesn't. We all respond differently to given events and I can tell you that 99% of the success of any endeavor has nothing to do with whatever program you're in; it has to do with you.

Discerning the Truth

We live in a world of sound bites, these days. People hear a five second statement and make all kinds of assumptions; some right, some wrong. This is especially true for those seeking direction and help with issues in their lives; they hear a statement and create a solution in their minds based on part of what they've heard. Then they're upset when it doesn't work.

One of the statements I hear very frequently comes from *The Secret*. People tell me that it says if you want something, you simply have to imagine that you already have it and it will be yours. Is this the truth? The answer is yes and no.

The Law of Attraction has been written and talked about extensively over the last few years. This law states that whatever you set your intentions on, or focus on, you'll get. So, that part is true. However, what's also true is that most of us have counter intentions in the form of limiting beliefs which interfere with the process. If you don't believe me, think back to last New Year's Day. Did you keep the resolution you made or did you give it a few weeks and then store the idea away like an old pair of socks? What about that goal to lose 20 pounds? Are you actually lighter or still wearing your fat jeans? What about that promise you made to your spouse to pay down your debt? Are you richer or did you just charge that new set of whitewalls? If all you had to do was set the intention, then you would have reached every single goal you have; yet, you didn't. Identifying and then clearing these counter intentions is a significant part of the equation.

So, does that mean if you clear the counter intentions from your mind, you can sit on the couch and wait for what you want to arrive? Absolutely not! You must take action. Opportunities will come to you that match your intentions, but if you never take a step, you won't see them. You never know how exactly your intention may be delivered, either. You have to remember that the universe has no blinders and delivers in completely unexpected ways. Just because you think you set the intention to make a million dollars investing in real estate, that doesn't necessarily mean you get the million dollars from that source. As you work on your real estate, you may be inspired to write an e-book that takes off or be asked to host your own television show that triples your income. The universe knows no restrictions and just delivers.

That's why this book is called *Expect Miracles*. It's the acknowledgement that we are constantly setting limits for ourselves. No matter what you call your understanding of a greater power; God, Buddha, Allah, the Universe or the Divine, that power knows no limits and stands at the ready to deliver miracles into our lives on a daily basis. If you set clear intentions and take action, you too, will experience miracles. The following story is a good example of what's possible when you clear your counter intentions and release the need to set limits in your life.

I first heard of the Law of Attraction through Joe's *Advanced Spiritual Marketing* e-book; though I had no clue after I read it what I'd really read and the impact that it could have on my life. As the saying goes, the teacher will come when the student is ready. When Joe's book, *The Attractor Factor*, came out in 2004 I read it and then knew beyond a shadow of a doubt what I had read. I was finally ready for the change that was about to happen in my life.

I put forth the intention to have the house I had wanted for the past five years. With bad credit and no idea how I was going to get it, I was a little skeptical. That was in October 2004. I began the steps set forth in the book and by November 28th, I had signed the contract for the purchase of the house. On December 7th 2004, we had moved in!

The amazing thing is, the day the owners moved out, some five years before, I had told them that the house was mine. Though I had no clue what I'd set forth that day, I had actually claimed the house as mine to the universe. The house had sold three times in that five years, but every time the buyer had defaulted. I kept telling the owners that the house was mine and I'd soon have it. Of course, they didn't believe me when I said it, but I knew without a doubt I would have the house when I was ready for that change in my life.

—Tonya Pruitt
http://www.vbcfire.com

There are a couple of things I want to point out about Tonya's story. First of all, it is a fabulous example of what you can accomplish when you really begin to expect miracles in your life. Second, it really illustrates how big the problem of counter intentions can be. Why did it take five years for Tonya's house to manifest when she'd obviously claimed it at the very beginning? She answered that herself, she wasn't ready. She noted that because she had bad credit and no idea how the house would ever be hers, it stopped the process. It was only when she released these counter intentions did the house become hers and it became hers within weeks.

So, what's keeping you from getting what you want? You are! You may say you want great relationships, a new house or a million dollars, BUT…it's the 'but' that's standing in your way. You don't really believe you can have it and the reasons are varied; from past bad experiences to fear. The reason doesn't matter as much as the fact that you are allowing it to get in your way. You're choosing to allow it to stop you, just as Tonya believed her credit would stop her. You have the power to choose differently and when you make that choice, life opens its possibilities up to help you get your heart's desire.

Another guru sound bite that I'm asked about frequently is "Just get over it." The concept being conveyed here is that if you've had problems or issues that continually get in your way, you should just get over them and move onto something that serves you better. I don't agree with this idea. Trying to gloss over the issues or pretend they don't exist is nothing more than lying to yourself. I have the same problem with those who say you should merely think positive. While a positive outlook can do wonders for your life, it's not the answer by itself. You must still do the hard work and look within yourself to clear the counter intentions before real progress can be made.

While I don't think you have to relive your traumatic experiences, you do have to acknowledge that they occurred and recognize the beliefs that you created because of them. Otherwise, you'll never be able to move on. You can fool yourself for awhile, but eventually something will trigger those beliefs and they'll come rushing back full force. Once you acknowledge your beliefs and their origin, you can then start recognizing your reactions and emotions to particular triggers and choose to create different beliefs.

The truth about all these guru ideas is that all of them have a small kernel of truth; it's the assumptions made about what that means that's confusing to people. Each and every one of us is inspired by the people we meet in our lives and those people can encourage us to be better versions of ourselves; that's a good thing.

So then, why are you still struggling? Why is it that you try various methods of accomplishing your goals only to fall short, yet again? One reason is the idea of control. We all like to think that we control our little corner of the world. To this end, we establish comfort zones, routines and boundaries that we may not even be conscious of. You may have built protective walls around your life that actually limit what you can accomplish and sabotage any attempt to move beyond them.

I've always considered myself a writer. When I was younger, I thought that in order to really be a writer, there had to be suffering involved—and boy, did I suffer! Creditors were calling, my old clunker car was barely running and I lived on peanut butter sandwiches. But I was a writer and I was supposed to struggle, right? Wrong. I had created in my head the story of what it means to be a writer; in other words, I had decided what it meant, rather than allowing for the possibilities of what it could be.

Every time it looked like I might do well with my writing and rise above the financial chaos in my life, I would do something to sabotage it. This was a very strong counter intention in my life and took me some time to really get clear and improve my situation.

Fear is not your Friend

Two of the strongest counter intentions you will combat are the fear of failure and the fear of success. The stories you connect with these events are what keep you within the comfort zone you know and prevent you from reaching your goals. You're afraid to be outside your barriers, even if you say you want it. So, as a result of this fear, you let go of the progress you've made; often never seeing your goals materialize.

In the early Star Wars movies, the Emperor didn't tolerate failure; to fail was an immediate death sentence. Some people feel that if you fail in the attempt to reach a certain goal, you're worthy of a form of death in a psychological sense. This 'all or nothing' mindset prevents you from understanding the positive direction that failure can offer. It's important to understand that failure doesn't mean the end. It's merely a clue that you've temporarily stepped off the path to your goal. It's a natural part of the education and learning process. We give something a try and then evaluate what went well and what needs improvement. This doesn't mean that it's useless to try again. It just gives us more information and knowledge for our next attempt. The actual act of failing is usually nothing earth shaking, yet the fear of failing and what that might say about you, is huge. Failure isn't the enemy, as it gives you good feedback and a new direction. The real enemy is fear.

In addition to the tendency to create stories about ourselves, we may create stories about others, as well, limiting the impact they can have on our lives. Many people fall into this trap with successful people or self-development gurus. They think, "Well, they can't really understand my situation or help me." Instantly, you've stopped any good that you might have gained from that person. It doesn't matter if you've already achieved some success in your life, you can still gain wonderful things from others if only you allow it.

Many of you will remember the Steven Spielberg movie *E.T.* Actress Dee Wallace starred in that movie and sent me her thoughts on how allowing the input of others had improved her life.

After reading *The Attractor Factor*, I realized I was dismissing people and opportunities because of various judgments (i.e. Their appearance, education, work standing, etc.). I immediately turned that around with the intention of allowing everything. Within a week, I had been invited to participate in a wonderful online seminar, to do a podcast for my upcoming book, *Conscious Creation* and I had received an offer from a CPA to find lost money, at no expense. I realized the miracle of allowing the universe to create; I just had to get out of the way.

—Dee Wallace
Actress, Author & Speaker
www.officialdeewallace.com

Dee's story points out the fact that we all have preconceived notions or stories in our minds about others. Once you become aware that these notions aren't serving you, you'll be able to set them aside and allow miracles to come to you.

Have you ever had the thought, "I'm a great starter, just not such a great finisher."? Do you have half-completed home remodeling projects, half a degree, or a pile of half-read books? It's frustrating, isn't it? Oftentimes, you'll make excuses for not doing what you set out to do, but all of those explanations fall short of not having the courage to actually get it done. What's the point of starting something and not finishing it? You know this is a waste of time and energy. Yet, you may do this repeatedly. Why? Because, whether you're conscious of it or not, you fear success and what that might mean in your life.

The fear of success is very common; more common than you might suspect. It almost seems backward to fear the very thing you say you want, but many people do. Even those individuals who achieve great success can squander their achievements and riches away due to this fear.

Fear is the anxiety of anticipation; in other words, it's the 'what if?' In reality, fear has only the meaning we give it. If we give it no meaning or if we allow something else to have greater meaning, then fear has little or no influence upon us. This is where expectation comes into play.

If you expect miracles in your life, then release any attachment to the outcome, you're allowing for the fulfillment of that expectation from any person or direction possible. Rather than insisting that success or achievement come from one specific avenue and fulfill only one expectation, you open up to all the universe has to offer.

Now, I want to make it perfectly clear that it doesn't have to be a big life altering goal that you want to achieve for this to work. Miracles come in small packages each and every day. Remember when you were a kid and stood in line to tell Santa exactly what you wanted? Your mind would race, trying to pick the biggest and most expensive gift you could imagine; you couldn't bother Santa with a small or insignificant wish. This isn't the same. These aren't just wishes; they're your new reality. By learning to clear your counter intentions and allow miracles into your life, you reap all the benefits, large and small. It doesn't have to be a year from now; it can happen today no matter where you are in your life. Jonathan Lagace is a great example.

> I'm a 20 year old college student and I've been using the law of
> attraction for the last few months, with excellent results. I was
> having some money problems; after I found out about the law of
> attraction I did some research and tried out some different ideas I
> found. Within a week of changing the way I think, I started receiving
> checks in the mail. Some I was expecting, like a check from the gov-
> ernment for GST/HST credit here in Canada. It was supposed to be
> for $60, but when I opened it, the check was for $237. Now I receive
> more checks than bills and it's great! Between the unexpected checks
> and my new booming internet business, I can now say that I'm well
> on my way to living the life I want to live. Since I've changed the way
> I think, everything has been better; business, family, and myself in
> general. Thanks Joe, you've really helped me open my eyes and let
> me see that anything is possible, if you think and believe.
>
> —Jonathan Lagace
> www.lagace-ebooks.com

It doesn't matter if you're 20 years old or 60, nor is it important if you've already achieved some success or are just starting out, as Jonathan is.

Have you ever found yourself in a situation where you witnessed someone just becoming successful or achieving a certain breakthrough and you thought to yourself, "I could never do that." Most of us prob-ably have; even successful people experience this feeling at some point in their lives. There are still things I want to accomplish and I occasionally have to clear away counter intentions or limiting beliefs, just like you do.

So how do you recognize a counter intention? Because many of these intentions are ingrained early in our development or experience, they can be hard to spot. I've listed a few of the most prevalent to help get you started; you'll probably recognize a few of them.

Counter Intentions 101

(1) I'm not good enough.

Many of us can remember standing in the school yard waiting to be picked for the team. No matter when you were finally picked, if you weren't picked first, you felt inferior. This process happens repeatedly throughout life; the job you didn't get, the relationship that dissolved, notice from the electric company that you're about to be shut off. It's hard to feel good about yourself when these events happen and you carry that feeling with you. Unfortunately, when you decide to change your life it can get in the way. That little voice in the back of your mind is telling you that you aren't good enough while you're doing all you can to reach your goals. It's like having one foot on the gas and the other on the brake at the same time.

(2) No one likes me.

Everyone has flaws and some people are more than willing to point them out at the worst times. You may think that you aren't well spoken or don't have perfect manners or you may feel like you don't really belong. It can be easy to assume that no one likes you, just because you don't have a large social network. However, like all counter intentions, this one is self fulfilling. Because you believe you don't deserve friends or relationships, you don't try to have them and therefore, you don't. Once you realize that this perception isn't the reality, you can take steps to reverse its effects.

(3) I don't want to be rejected.

This is a common counter intention that affects many people from all walks of life. It exists in a student who is fearful of asking the teacher for assistance, a worker asking a colleague for help and especially in a person trying to ask another person for a date. This counter intention is driven primarily by fear. No one wants to be rejected, but the fear of rejection is often much larger than the actual event. Only you can decide not to allow it to interfere with your plans.

(4) That's impossible!

There are things that are possible and things that we believe are possible *for us*. These are frequently very different. While you may realize that the goals you want for your life have been accomplished repeatedly by many others, you may put them in the impossible category because you feel you lack the qualities, knowledge, tools, or resources necessary to accomplishing them. This is actually connected to the first counter intention that I discussed; you don't feel good enough. This is how you sort goals or tasks in life into the 'can do' or 'can't do' list. This happens automatically on a subconscious level and will frequently cause you to reject ideas before they are even considered.

(5) Tunnel Vision

People with this counter intention believe that there is only one solution to a particular problem or that there's only one way to perform a certain task. For example, you may think that the only way to really make money is to get a good education, get a good job and work your way up the corporate ladder. But, many self employed people are making excellent money. If your response starts with, 'Yeah, but…' then you have this counter intention and believe that things can only happen in one way for you and it has to be a specific way. What this does is limit all the other avenues that may be viable ways for you to reach your goals. You're saying that other methods are viable for someone else, but for some reason they won't work for you.

(6) It's not going to work, anyway.

This is one of the most damaging counter intentions anyone can have and sadly, it's very prevalent. These are the people who constantly see the worst; almost as if they're trying to protect themselves from getting their hopes up. Often these people believe that whatever they do will fail, so they don't try or only give it a very half-hearted try. Again this is a self fulfilling prophecy; they fail not because it was inevitable but because they believed it was so. It can be hard not to be skeptical when trying something new. However, if you allow this counter intention to remain, you'll repeatedly fail; thereby reinforcing this belief.

(7) I'm not special.

This counter intention is the basic belief that success requires some special quality or spark that you don't have. It's the feeling that you're just average and it's too much to expect that you accomplish anything great. This belief that you're not 'chosen' allows you to escape the responsibilities of making the right choices for your life. You're ultimately responsible for your success, but with this counter intention, it can be easier to find something or someone to blame rather than making the choices required to bring about your own success.

While this is a short list it gives you a good idea of the kind of hindrances that counter intentions can cause in your own life. In the next chapter, we'll talk about getting clear and what techniques can help you get past the counter intentions in your life. But first, I'd like to share with you a couple of stories that illustrate what's possible when you are able to remove counter intentions and self-limiting beliefs and allow the miracles that await you to flow into your life.

Maria Beale Fletcher represents how far you can go when you decide what's possible and that you deserve to reach your goals.

Creating miracles using Dr. Joe Vitale's process from the *Attractor Factor*, reminds me of a game my beloved Scottish grandmother taught me when I was four. Grandma would say, "Send out a good thought and another good thought will return in its place. Send out a bad thought and a bad thought replaces it. The trick is, Maria, to be very careful in creating the thoughts you send out. When you're excited about good thoughts and they make you happy, then you know you're playing the game to win!"

When I was nine years old, I watched *What's My Line* on our neighbor's television with my family. A beautiful, glamorous woman with an accent was the Mystery Guest. The distinguished panel of four, blindfolded celebrities couldn't guess her identity. She was a famous European movie star. Jumping up with excitement, I decided that one day I, too would be famous and would appear as the beautifully dressed Mystery Guest on *What's My Line*. The next day after school, as I was practicing my accent in the mirror, I was taken by surprise when my eight-year-old sister walked in on me and insisted on knowing what I was doing. When I told her, she wanted to know what I would be famous for. "I don't know," I said, "All I know is that I'll be famous and when the time comes to be on the show, I must be ready with my disguise."

In high school, I was determined to become a Rockette so I finished my schooling in three years. At the suggestion of the Jaycees and because I was interested in scholarship money for college, I competed in the Miss Asheville Pageant. Two weeks later, as the new Miss Asheville, my parents put me on a train for New York City to audition for the Radio City Music Hall Rockettes. This was even after learning from Russell Markert, the dance director at the Music Hall that there wouldn't be an audition for another two years! But he was kind enough to take my father's phone number and told us that if anything happened; he'd call.

Something happened! One of the Rockettes got sick and I was her size! Six weeks after arriving in New York City, I passed the private audition. I performed as a Rockette in the Christmas show, *Parade of the Wooden Soldiers*. After seven months, I took a leave of absence to compete in the Miss North Carolina Pageant. At my surprise farewell party, the Rockettes crowned me Miss America 1962 four months *before* I competed for the title in Atlantic City, New Jersey. The significance of that moment allowed me to pretend I was already Miss America when Bert Parks introduced me as Miss North Carolina and every time I had to compete on stage.

Twenty-four hours after I was crowned Miss America 1962, I appeared on *What's My Line* as the Mystery Guest. Just before I walked onstage in my evening gown with my new Miss America crown on my 19-year-old head, my chaperone asked me if I was nervous. "No," I said. "I rehearsed for this appearance ten years ago and I'm ready to go out there with my disguise." She looked stunned!

Fast forward to March 2007 and I'm mesmerized, watching the movie, *The Secret*, starring Dr. Joe Vitale and other speakers. I started buying and reading Dr. Vitale's books. Six months later, I signed up for his Online Miracles class, coached by Lee Follender. I decided to take action and to control, once again, my thinking; eliminating the bad habits I had slipped into over the years. Instead,

I chose to be grateful for everything that showed up in my life, even the bad stuff! During the course, I made a decision to recreate the faith I exhibited as the nine-year-old girl I once was.

By using the process, I learned from my grandmother and Dr. Joe Vitale and by not being attached to the outcome, I received miracles. I became what I visualized. I became Miss America. I became a Rockette and I became that Mystery Guest. I used my Miss America scholarship to study French and Philosophy at Vanderbilt University and in Aix-en-Provence, France. More recently, I found a residual income, creating a business I love doing in which I use talents I thought were deeply buried. I celebrate my freedom to travel in my new business and to ski and visit my grandchildren frequently.

—Maria Beale Fletcher—former Miss America 1962
www.incomesecretthanksyoubigtime.com

I love Maria's story and I would have loved to meet her grandmother! One of the most striking points that Maria makes is that even if you experience great success in one area of your life and then stop using the tools available, you can still return to these ideas to get started again. It's never too early and never too late; you can pick up or resume at literally any point in your life.

It's equally important to understand that you can't be connected to the outcome. You can't have tunnel vision and insist that what you want be delivered in a certain way and according to your specifications. Occasionally, divine inspiration will show you the way and when it does, you should pounce on the opportunity. That's exactly what happened to Julie.

I've tried manifesting many times, many ways; with some success. But, often, it fell short of my dreams or the process wasn't all that much fun. I always felt like I was trying to make it happen; keep my vision just right, focus enough and hold my vibration high. In Joe's book, *Zero Limits*, he talks about coming from inspiration and I recently had an experience that truly comes from that place. What a difference!

I'm a builder and the local Homebuilders Association hosted a "Learn about Green Building" event that one of my clients attended with me. They talked about the upcoming National Green Building Conference and that some of the local homes that were built or remodeled green would be on the green home tour. I didn't know a thing about building green, but I had an 'I've GOT to do this' feeling. I felt so inspired. My client was inspired too, insisting that her house be on the tour.

Now, there were plenty of reasons to talk myself out of doing anything. First, I didn't know the first thing about green building. Second, her house is a small, 100-year-old, shotgun style; hardly the profile of a green house, which are usually modern and new. But, I followed the bread crumbs, so to speak and now this house has been totally renovated green and is on the tour! Everything just fell into place; the right people advised me, the normal renovation process went smoothly and the house is amazing. This project has also gained a great deal of local media attention; now they call me.

In addition to the tour and the great experience with the house, I've learned so much along the way, which I absolutely love. I've become a Certified Green Professional. Also, there isn't much information out there about how to renovate an old house in a green way, so I've started writing articles and maybe, a book to share what I've learned. I don't know where it's going, if anywhere beyond its current point, but this really is how we're meant to create. We don't have to make it happen. Creation happens to us. Taking inspired action from there is easy.

—Julie Groth
www.StepByStepConstructionCo.com

Now, if Julie had decided that her success as a builder had to be by building new homes of a particular type, in a new development somewhere, she might have never seen the opportunity that building green provided. By following the inspiration and letting it lead her, she was able to attract all the help she needed to learn how to make the house a showcase of green building.

It might have been easier for Julie to say, "No, I don't know anything about building green; it's not my thing." But she would have completely missed what is turning out to be her particular calling and niche as a builder.

CHAPTER 2

The Search for Clarity

In order to send your intentions out into the universe and expect miracles, you have to understand how the law of attraction helps you and what steps are necessary to speed up the process. I'm asked frequently what the difference is between expecting miracles and using the law of attraction. They actually work in harmony. My assistant Suzanne has a great way of explaining how they complement each other.

Oftentimes, when we hear the word 'miracle', we think in really big, outlandish terms, whereby we imagine such Hollywood ideas of a cloud formation in the sky transforming itself into a hand and swooping down to rescue a baby from a burning car at the last minute. Others would say that a miracle involves overcoming the incurable and the impossible. My favorite definition of a miracle comes from Marianne Williamson quoting *A Course in Miracles*; she states that "A miracle is a shift in perception." Meaning that as soon as we modify our thoughts from fear to love, things instantly change and a miracle occurs. Author Paul Ferrini says that we are always just one thought away from feeling good again. Wouldn't you say that it's a powerful gesture to be in control of your own state of mind and deciding how you wish your emotions to be affected?

One of life's secrets is that if you're experiencing something you don't like, it means that inside yourself, you're blocked and as soon as you release the obstacle, in an instant, everything begins to shift and fall into place in a loving, perfect way and most often, in ways you hadn't expected and fortunately, always for the better.

In essence, the Law of Attraction is in complete alignment with the miracle process. Considering that miracles are synonymous with wonder, marvel or an event manifesting, The Law of Attraction works by responding to your thoughts and feelings, thus the Universe rearranges itself around you, allowing you to have the experiences you created.

There are so many techniques available to us in order to manifest the life of our dreams. Personally, I have always had great success writing things down. Whenever I wish to experience something, I write it down by hand. I state it in the positive, act as if I already have it and then let it go and completely forget about it. I'm not worried about how it will come to me, but I stay in the present, feeling joyful about the process and knowing that my desires are on their way and I'm excited to see just how it will all come about.

—Suzanne Burns
www.IntentionalTreasures.com

I've written numerous books and one of the first that I wrote that dealt with the idea of getting clear and using the law of attraction was *The Attractor Factor*. The Law of Attraction is very powerful and in order to allow it to work in your life you must follow certain steps. These steps are:

1. **Remove negativity and focus on what you want**
   This means to stop focusing on the negative events in your life. Stop gossiping and repeating every bad story you hear. How often have you encountered someone who never has a good thing to say about anything or anyone? It can be very draining and you don't want to be that person or even be around them! One of the basic truths about the law of attraction is that it can work for you as well as against you. If you focus on what you want and do everything you can to keep positive words and thoughts around you, you'll see positive things happen. However, if you dwell on the negative and are always whining and worrying about what you don't have, you will just attract more negativity.

2. **Dare something worthy**
   When was the last time you tried something new or made a decision that really excited you or got your imagination running wild? Was it the prospect of a new business deal or taking a relationship to the next level or just meeting someone that had a real impact on your thinking? Even when you're setting goals and plodding along in life, you have to ask yourself, are these really worthy goals? Because we all

have self-limiting beliefs about what we can each achieve, it's common to set goals we know we can meet. While this is still good, it doesn't push you into unknown territory and get you excited. When you set a goal that you have no clue how to meet, you're evoking the full power of the law of attraction; you're daring to dream of something that is truly worthy of you.

3. **Get clear**

You must remove any counter intentions before you will be able to move forward. This is an internal understanding of why you feel the way you do in certain situations. One of the easiest and most obvious ways to spot a counter intention is to notice when you have an emotional reaction to something. Did a comment or situation make you angry or sad? If so, then those emotions must be investigated. It's not until they're exterminated that you will be able to reach your goals and you must hunt them down with persistence, as they will most likely try to rear their ugly heads many times in your life.

4. **Nevillize your goal**

Neville Goddard set forth the idea that you should act as if you have already received what you want. This means to visualize it in your mind and feel it with strong emotion. Emotion has a great deal of power and allows you to focus your energy. It is this energy that will allow you to see the paths and possibilities of reaching your goals. Now remember, this visualization is not your run-of-the-mill imagining. It is the kind of visualizing that you can almost feel, touch, smell and taste. If you want a new home, you must visualize it to the last detail. Imagine yourself standing on the back porch, breathing in the scent of honeysuckle as the sun goes down. Picture your family around the dining room table, carving a thanksgiving turkey. Can you smell the sage dressing and gravy? That's Nevillizing; attaching an emotion so strong you can feel it in every part of your being.

5. **Let go**

Letting go means just that. It may seem ridiculous that after all this planning and visualizing, you are now expected to let it go, but that's the only way to get it. It sounds like I'm talking in circles, doesn't it? Think back to what I said about tunnel vision; hanging onto the outcome and expecting it to come a certain way only reduces the number of paths it can take. You must let go and trust that you'll be shown the way and you will receive what you envisioned.

These steps will allow you to get anything you desire. Right; so why isn't it working? You been thinking positive and rejecting all that negative chatter. You've also envisioned a really worthy goal that gets your motor running and blood pumping. You've visualized it for hours on end, so where the heck is it, already?

Have you really gotten clear? Have you addressed all those beliefs and voices that say you're not good enough or that you might fail? If you aren't making progress, then you probably haven't. It is, by far, the hardest part of the entire process.

Following is a short list of questions to get you started in the process. Remember, whenever you have an emotional reaction to an event or person you can use these questions to start your investigation.

Getting Clear

What just happened? Describe the person or event you just reacted to.

_____

For example, someone you work with or are related to, teases you, but you perceive that they are attacking you or making you look bad. You may even get angry at them and tell them to back off. This means that you may think people deliberately try to make you look bad. Now answer the next question.

Here is how I reacted to the situation or event or person.

_____

When it happened, I felt angry, sad, fearful…

_____

Now, read over what you've just written. Try to take an objective look at what happened. Was your reaction really justified? Why or why not? Why did it make you emotional?

_____

What are you afraid might happen in this situation? What does it say about you?

_____

Can you think about a time when you started thinking this was an issue? When did you decide that this was your story?

_____

What choice will you make to change the story you tell yourself?

_____

If this were to happen again, how might you perceive the event?

_____

_____

How might your reaction be different?

_____

_____

Now, think about what happened. What kind of experience did it create for you and those around you? Write this down with sentences beginning with 'I' which allow you to take responsibility.

I _____

I _____

I _____

I _____

The story I created for myself makes me feel:

_____

The best way to get clear is to identify the issue and then make a plan to change that perception or belief. Once you do that, you're able evaluate your emotions and understand why those happened in the first place. Then, you can replace those emotions with ones that will serve you better. You're able to choose your new beliefs and put them into place.

Now comes the most important part. You must release that old belief. Say to yourself:

I am now willing, ready and I fully choose for this old belief,

_____ ,

to be completely and 100% released.

In its place, I am willing and allow myself to have this perception

_____

and I believe that _____.

I now allow myself to feel_____.

This is just a start and lets you go through the entire process. I find that often, people will start to look inside and evaluate what caused the beliefs behind their emotional responses and not like what they see. They may deny the cause and refuse to deal with it or change it. Don't misunderstand me; I don't think you have to relive traumatic events, but you do need to see them for what they created in your life and take responsibility for your current choices.

Don't be that person who harbors anger or sadness like a familiar cloak. The comfort these past bad events give you is misplaced and continues to affect your future. Only by releasing the emotion attached to the past, can you get clear and move on to what awaits you.

The Trial of the Century

You can think of the process of clearing like a police investigation and trial. First, you pay attention to the clues that point to the perpetrator (your counter intentions) and also identify any accomplices (limiting beliefs). Then, it's time for the interrogation. You must quiz these ideas and get to the real truth. You don't let up and you don't let them off the hook. You need to ask the hard questions: what, where, when, how and why?

Once you have your evidence, take it to court and present your case. You are the judge and jury. Is this idea (now in handcuffs and an orange jumpsuit) the truth or is it fear in disguise? Is it what you want for your life or isn't it? You decide. You can choose to release this idea back into your life or to get rid of it forever. Once you decide that the idea must go, you present your closing arguments which outline exactly what you do want and how you will achieve it. These closing arguments are detailed and emotional. Finally, the bailiff takes the culprit away and you walk out into freedom.

Visualizing this process in your mind allows you to imagine all the steps necessary to get clear. I especially like the idea of putting the counter intention or limiting belief on trial. You don't bury it or pretend it's not there. You examine and question it to get to the real truth.

Once you go through the clearing process, you may find that your belief is a result of a negative or unfortunate event. Everyone has experiences that can easily be viewed as negative and I'm no exception. But you choose how it affects you. Let me give you an example of how this works.

Five years ago, I co-signed a loan for my then web guy to get a car. I had never co-signed for anyone and I'll probably never do it again. But the experience was useful for me and in a moment it will be useful for you, too. Over the years, he would miss car payments and I'd get a call from his bank. Then I'd have to find him, bail him out financially, and hope the situation improved.

It didn't.

A few months ago, his bank called again. This time, they said they couldn't find my web guy (who was by then no longer working for me) at all and that he was several *months* past due. The bank was demanding complete payment of the loan. *Right away*. I began to search for the guy who had skipped out on the car loan. I called every number I had for him and wrote every email address I'd ever known him to use and searched online. I even had my chief assistant spend time shaking trees to see if he would fall out of one of them.

Nothing.

One of my closest advisers said, "He's gone. You'll never find him. If you did find him, you'd never get a dime out of him. Pay off the loan to close the case and protect your credit." I agreed and paid off the loan. I wasn't upset. I wasn't concerned. I just let it go and kept clearing on any negative thoughts that came up. I let it go and attached no emotion to the event. Then a curious thing happened.

My old web guy contacted me on Facebook, asking to be my friend! I instantly let him in. I also wrote him and asked for his phone number. He knew why I wanted it. He wrote back, gave me his number, said he was sorry and that he would do anything for me to resolve the issue. He also said he didn't have any money.

I had already made peace with the situation, so I didn't really have an attachment to any outcome. I figured if I could get him to create a website or two for me, I'd let it all go and chalk it up to experience. He agreed and created a wonderful site and even a wonderful sales letter for it. But he also did something else that stunned everyone around me, but just made me smile.

He sent me a cashier's check for the full amount he owed me; about six thousand dollars! He also said he would continue to do work for me, gratis, to show his good faith. No one around me could believe it. I had found the guy who skipped town. He did work for me *and* he paid me off.

How did this happen?

First, I wasn't attached to him paying me back. I would *welcome* my money back, but I didn't need it. Too many people want something to happen in their lives, but are desperate about it. That desperation creates/attracts more to be desperate about. I was okay whether the guy paid me or not. My energy was neutral.

Second, I saw the good in the guy and he felt that. I know that people at their core are basically good. They *want* to be good. Sometimes, when they're backed into a corner, they do things they regret. But I knew the guy and felt he was a good soul. He would try to be good in whatever way he could.

These two steps don't guarantee that you'll get your money back from someone who borrowed or stole from you, but they do guarantee *you* will be at peace with the moment. It's from that place of inner peace that you can attract what you desire; even if it's from someone who skipped town, couldn't be found and was flat broke.

You may say, 'well, that's how it happened for you, but how do you know it will happen for me?' Let me give you another example. I know a woman named Tara who had been through a traumatic divorce. I've never experienced a divorce, but I know it can be very hard to trust again and release the anger and hurt. Tara describes her experience this way:

I'd had it. I mean, really, I was done! Dating? No more. It was too hard and too heartbreaking. I couldn't attract the right kind of man and I prefer to be alone than with someone that doesn't fit. Allergy shots were in my future so I could become the stereotypical single woman with cats.

It was February, 2007 and I was disillusioned. Divorced for three years, I hadn't been in a relationship for months. I like the break to be sure of what I felt about my situation and that I was okay. I knew I needed to recover, to heal and to clear my head. I went online and even joined a singles group. I was lucky in life, as other areas seemed to be going well, yet still unlucky in love.

A male friend even went so far as to suggest that I was 'undate-able' and said I shouldn't date, since I didn't want to move in with someone, get married and have babies in the short-term. I disagreed; though the criticism made me wonder if this friend was right.

Finally, I was inspired! Having spent the past three years watching *The Secret* and reading everything from *The Attractor Factor* to *Zero Limits* to *The Success Principles*, I decided it was time to take action.

I decided to act as if I had the perfect boyfriend. I called him 'Mr. Wonderful'; it fit him. He was kind, thoughtful, supportive, a great communicator and boy, did he 'flip my switch'. He was truly perfect in every way.

I told my sister and a few friends about him. It was wonderful to have this man in my life. They started asking me questions, which helped me to fine tune.

"Does he plan trips? Like, does he do the research, make the reservations, everything?"

"Of course!" I replied. "As a matter of fact, we're going off for a romantic getaway this weekend!" As they quizzed me, he evolved.

Then, one magical night in April, I attended a dinner theater event with the singles group I had joined. I sat next to Craig, a man I had met back in October. We had always been friendly, but never dated. I didn't get that 'interested' vibe from him. But this night would change things.

I helped Craig win two tickets to a basketball game and without thinking, asked where we were sitting; I'm not shy. That game was destined to be the beginning of a wonderful relationship the likes of which I never dreamt possible. He's everything I ever wanted and things I never knew I could have. I'm thankful for him every day when my feet hit the floor and every night when my head hits the pillow.

'Mr. Wonderful' came and his name is Craig. I 'willed him to be so.' I am forever grateful for the skills I've learned from the likes of Joe Vitale. I believe in the power of universal energy and I stand, arms wide open and ask, "What next?"

—Tara Reed
www.tarareeddesigns.com

It would have been easy for Tara to use her divorce as an excuse to hide herself away. She also could have allowed her friend's criticism to hurt her and keep her out of circulation. Instead, she released those negative events and chose to focus on what she did want. She imagined her dream match in extreme detail and attracted exactly what she'd been looking for.

But wait a minute; didn't she just convince herself that this was the guy she imagined? No! Absolutely not. She didn't take the first hunk of burning love that came along. She created her result in her mind. This is how she was able to recognize him when he appeared and pass up all the others. She knew what she was looking for, so of course she found it.

I like to think of clearing as a life-long process that is much like peeling an onion. You dig down through each layer, some thinner and some thicker and don't stop for your whole life.

Finding Your Direction

How can you expect your intention to arrive if you don't even know what it is? I frequently hear from people who are in the position of not being exactly sure what they want. That's when you can allow inspiration to take hold. One of my favorite stories is about the Cavanaughs. Donna and her husband were in their mid-forties with the second phase of their life just beginning.

Recently, my husband and I stepped into the world of empty nesters. We were in our mid-forties and our only child was going off to college. While we were excited about this stage of life, we were also apprehensive about what our future held. So, we did what any other couple would do in our situation, we headed to Atlantic City.

While there, I saw an ad for *The Secret*. At first, I scoffed at the principles behind the work, but my curiosity got the better of me. I ordered the DVD and almost immediately, we were enveloped by a feeling of what the Law of Attraction could mean for our lives.

A few months later, we were watching an NFL playoff game. A disastrous decision by one of the coaches inspired my computer engineering husband to develop a statistic that could help coaches know ahead of time if their plays had a significant chance of success. Let me confess right here that I have often tuned out my husband's engineering talk, but something hit me this time and I remembered a scene from *The Secret* that spoke about taking action when inspiration hits.

I began to ask him questions and before we knew it, we had mapped out how his statistic could not only help coaches, but fans, fantasy football players and broadcasters. I told him this was an idea we had to act on.

We had no experience of, or knowledge about, starting a business, but I contacted a lawyer to find out how we could patent and trademark his stat. We named the stat *PossessionPoints*® and incorporated our web-based enterprise to form *PossessionPoints.com*; a site that analyzes game statistics and projects NFL winners and losers. The ideas continued and my husband developed another form of the stat that offered a novel way of selecting Fantasy Football players.

We couldn't believe we'd embarked on this path. With each step, I held on to the idea that I should just trust in the Universe. We struggled the first season as we worked to get subscribers to our website. I worked the business end, while my husband worked on the mathematics. I got him booked on sports radio stations and I spoke at entrepreneurial forums. Neither of us had done any public speaking before, but here we were, talking football statistics with audiences.

There were still struggles, but with each obstacle, a solution came. When we realized we needed more money to grow the company the way we wanted, we looked for ways to make this happen. A little voice told me to look into venture capital. I had no idea how it worked, but I learned and this season, we will have our funding and grow *PossessionPoints*® into the company we've envisioned. This has been an amazing ride for us. One day, I'm a football widow and a year later, I'm CEO of a company that analyzes the NFL. I can honestly say I never saw this coming.

—Donna Cavanaugh
www.possessionpoints.com

One important point to note in Donna's story is that they didn't have a plan, but they were open to ideas. Once that idea appeared, they took action. No matter what stage of life you're in or whether or not you're sure of your direction, being able to see the opportunities when they appear is key. If you're still battling with emotions brought about by the past, you may never recognize new opportunities and they will pass you by.

I will offer a short word of caution; sometimes if you say you want something, but aren't very clear about the result you're after; it can be mixed. The following is a short example I received from Gary Boudurant.

When I first learned of the Law of Attraction I decided it was time for a new car. At the time, I was driving a 1989 VW Fox that had seen better days. The driver's side door handle was busted from a break in, so I had to open it by reaching across from the passenger's side; the radiator leaked and so on. But it got me around, mostly. However, I was determined to get a different car!

My choice was a four-door, silver VW Golf and I wanted it free. So I wrote about it, visualized driving it, talked about it and every time I saw one, which got more frequent, I told everyone that it was my car! After six months, my sister called me and asked if I would like a car for my birthday! I know what you're thinking; but honestly, I hadn't told anyone in my family about the law of attraction, it just wasn't in their mental framework.

Here's what I got for my birthday; a new-to-me, free, 4-door, silver Ford! Get this, the exterior driver's side door handle didn't work and there was a small leak in the radiator hose. The lesson; be very specific and clear about what you want.

—Gary Boudurant
http://www.investworks.net

This example always brings a smile to my face. Gary is exactly right; he got what he asked for, nothing more and nothing less. He didn't visualize a car in perfect working order; just that it be silver and different from his current ride and that's what he got. So be very careful what you say you want!

Ego and Divine Intentions

Before we get too far, it's important to discuss Intentions. Intentions are what you put out into the universe as your goal. They are what you say you want. There are two types of intentions, ego intentions and divine intentions. Ego intentions are things such as a new car or lots of cash in the bank. They are things that make you feel better about yourself and your life.

Divine intentions are those which carry an idea of a greater good. They help others as well as you. A divine intention might be to create ideas and concepts that help others reduce the emotional chaos in their lives. By helping them get what they want and need, you get what you want and need, as well. Wealth and riches are secondary.

One of the principles of evoking the power of the law of attraction is to dare something worthy. The more worthy the goal, the more it concentrates this power and attracts results much faster. In effect, it supercharges the law of attraction.

At one time, I was a struggling, starving writer in Houston, just trying to make ends meet. I'd had a very modest amount of success and started teaching classes at a local college. I really think that is what lit the fuse, so to speak and made me realize that I liked helping others get what they want. Yes, I wanted money in the bank. Yes, I wanted to make a name for myself and write more books. What I found was that by helping others and encouraging them along their path, the money and recognition flowed almost effortlessly. This started a cycle of learning and understanding and over the years, as I discovered things that helped my own life, I shared them. Everything that I'd ever wanted, a nice car, a beautiful home in the hill country and recognition in a global environment have come to pass because I set out the divine intention to help others.

I'm not saying that it's wrong to want a new car or to see some other small miracle manifest in your life. These are great ways to confirm that you're on the right path and to encourage you to take the next step. But, it also indicates how much more is waiting for you and what else is possible.

Let's take the example of Ebony. She had an idea for a business that benefits children.

I was inspired by Joe Vitale on *The Secret*. Then, I went online and signed up for his newsletter. At that time, everything in my mind was cluttered and I had no real direction; I didn't know whether I wanted to go back to corporate America or start my own business. I jotted down in my journal a vision that I'd had; a kids' party place where the kids would ride pedal rides, to get kids moving again. They could have fun and get fit at the same time! I visualized numerous locations. I was able to see it, smell it, and hear the laughter of children enjoying themselves and kids crying, not wanting to leave my party place. I visited my parents for Easter '07 and on my six-and-a-half hour drive back to Desoto, Texas, I wrote my business plan.

Everything was so clear because I was following Joe's steps. In my journal, I sketched a roadway with colors and vivid details and I felt wonderful. Then, I knew I had to react because the universe loves speed. I found a location and signed the lease on Friday, April 13, 2007. I started attracting everything I required to launch the business, from the building contractor to bring my vision to reality, to an 80K line of credit at the bank. Three months later, on July 18, 2007, I opened the doors to Ride N Zone.

I have hosted all-inclusive, private, themed birthday parties, field trips and open play sessions which consist of thousands of kids, parents and grandparents. The model works, guests love the concept and I'm ready to spread the word beyond my community. I became clear on the direction required and began manifesting what I needed to spread the word. Thus, began my next spiritual journey.

I submitted an entry on February 28, 2008, for the Hewlett Packard contest to build your brand, '*HP What Do You Have To*

Say'. Within a couple of weeks, I received the information that
I had won first place. The same week I entered the HP contest,
I wrote an email to the local Dallas morning show and told the
anchor that the 'Mompreneur' segment was on target and that I had
also taken that leap of faith and attracted everything required to get
my business up and running, by listening to that voice inside. She
loved my email and scheduled me as a guest to feature my business
and my story on *Good Morning Texas*.

   I have also received over ten offers to license or franchise my
business. This is the next phase of my journey. I have an inner
peace about myself and I am attracting people and things to me and
sometimes I don't even have to say a word. The good things just
come to me.

—Ebony Martin
www.rideNzone.com

Ebony chose a divine intention and the speed and power came, creating a miracle in her life. You can do the same; it's all up to you. Some
people have so many immediate needs that choosing a divinely inspired
intention can seem very far away. It can be a step-by-step process where
your immediate needs are attracted first and then you open your life to
the miracles that are yours. You may be in this situation yourself and have
trouble seeing how you can possibly wish for a miracle when you're just
trying to survive. You may be able to relate to the story of Rachel; a single
mom just trying to get by.

I've been divorced for the last two years; a single parent with two
sons. I have a great job at a university, but I still couldn't seem to
make ends meet, financially. Things got really bad and one day the
water was shut off. I begged and borrowed to get it turned back
on. I spent many days in a panic over money and wondered what I
was going to do to get by. Then, I came across *The Secret* online and
I started to do some research on the Law of Attraction. I eventually
scraped enough money together to buy the DVD, which I watched
almost daily for weeks.

   I started with the intentions and mentally, and what felt like
physically, pulled what I wanted toward me. A part time job came

to me, which helped in the short run, but wasn't the ideal solution to my problem. I bought Joe's book, *The Key* and I started to tell myself over and over again.... I love you....I forgive you.... I am sorry. Not really knowing for what, specifically, but it was the clearing I needed to receive money easily and not have to work so hard at two jobs for it. Within two months, I got a $12,000.00 raise from the university because of a grant that our department had submitted. I didn't know that my boss had written anything extra into that grant for my salary; it just came to me out of the blue. It was the money I needed to make ends meet and for me to relax for a change. I quit my second job so I would have more time with my children.

I kept working on the intention of money, although I had a little now. I never wanted to wait until I was desperate again. Plus, it's so much easier to attract what you want when you're not desperate and scared. I set out an intention to be a writer and to make some extra money doing that. But first, I had to do something to make that happen. Intentions only work if you do something toward making it happen. I wrote a couple of articles and submitted them to a club magazine. They bought the articles and offered to pay me $250 an article. I then suggested a "How To" book for the magazine to sell as a supplement. They enthusiastically responded by asking me to put a proposal together for them to look at. I'm so excited and thank Joe Vitale every day for giving me the tools to clear my mind, in order for the law of attraction to work.

—Rachel Anderson

CHAPTER 3

Creating Your Story

I wrote a book several years ago, called *Zero Limits*, that included a tremendously powerful clearing technique called Ho'oponopono. I discovered it when I met a man named Dr. Ihaleeakala Hew Len. Dr. Hew Len used Ho'oponopono in his practice which is the idea that you're responsible for everything that's in your life; no matter what you perceive to be the source. It reveals that only by loving yourself can you accept responsibility and change your life through cleansing and healing your higher self.

This is accomplished simply by repeating the phrases:

I love you.
I'm sorry.
Please forgive me.
Thank You.

This technique allows you to continually clear the thoughts, emotions and events that keep you from reaching that place of zero limits. This work is completely internal and can profoundly impact people and events that you don't even have direct contact with. Dr. Hew Len experienced this when he was treating patients at Hawaii State Hospital. By focusing on each patient and clearing with the ho'oponopono phrases the patients were healed from their mental problems without even having contact with the doctor.

What? That's the most frequent question I get when I talk about this technique and quite honestly it took me quite a while to wrap my head around the idea. The basic idea is the acceptance of everything that is in your life. Instead of pushing things off on others or blaming circumstance, you take responsibility for it. You first remind yourself that you are worthy of love and that love allows you to ask forgiveness for and release the events in your life. It is only through accepting total responsibility that you can attract true miracles to you.

I've been practicing this technique for a few years now and I have to say it's one of the most powerful I've ever encountered, which is why I dedicated an entire book to the idea. The Ho'opononpono technique compounds the miracles in your life tenfold and can astound you by promoting changes in you and others where you thought no changes were possible. These changes aren't restricted to big, earth shattering miracles, they can also represent very small, but no less significant shifts that can shock and amaze.

Evie's story is just one example.

I was at the supermarket where I always shop. They have one cashier that I avoid like the plague because she's unfriendly, brash and slow. This day, she was the only one working and I had to be in the very long line in front of her register to pay for my groceries. I was just finishing your book, *Zero Limits* and I thought, 'I'll try it out.' So I did. I said, "I love you; I'm sorry; please forgive me; thank you!" repeatedly in my mind until it was my turn with the cashier. She took my basket, emptied it, made a nice comment about my hair, smiled and even made a joke. The man behind me said to her, "What's going on with you? Why are you so friendly today?"

The woman replied, "I wasn't. I was in a foul mood, until now. I have no idea what's gotten into me. This isn't like me, is it?" Everybody nodded and I just hoped her cheerfulness would last the whole day.

—Evie Sullivan, Los Angeles

Now, you may look at this and say that it's a very small moment in one person's day and it is. But think how many of these small moments we must deal with and how they affect us. If you have the power to create a positive experience, then why wouldn't you do it? Simply by not reacting, taking responsibility and knowing you can affect your own outlook as well as that of others, you begin to understand the true power behind this ancient knowledge.

No matter where or who you are, there will be adverse things that happen during the course of a day. When confronted with these events, immediately using this technique will allow you to release the event and open yourself up to the good in the situation. Some of the most irritating people I encounter are those who intentionally goad me to try and get a reaction. This happened awhile back to a friend of mine, Anthony Tee-garden. Anthony is the author of a popular blog, as am I, and he relates this story of a very nasty email he received from one of his 'admirers'.

I was inspired to take up blogging on personal development since seeing Joe in *The Secret*. I have zero past writing experience, but figured I just needed to start and I'd get good as I went. Well, I recently received my very first, extremely negative email from a gentleman about my blogging, my grammar and my personal development philosophies in general. I was quite taken aback by his very personal attack, but by using one of the clearing methods from the book *The Key* and repeating to myself, "I love you, please forgive me…" from the book *Zero Limits*, I didn't react to this situation. I cleared and left myself open to inspiration about what to do next.

After clearing, I found myself copying the negative email into my blog and I started typing. Somehow, I knew I had to turn this into a win/win situation for myself and my subscribers without attacking this unhappy individual. I just started typing. In the end, I posted the nasty email to show my subscribers that 'dogs don't bark at parked cars'; however, something magical happened instead.

I realized by the end of the post that the universe was telling me to acknowledge and share all the positive emails that I'd received with my subscribers! I actually publicly *thanked* this gentleman for his email because without it, I wouldn't have realized I was keeping all of those positive emails to myself and not sharing their blessings with others! Below is the post:

Success Blog

Well it finally happened. I got my first nasty email about my blog today. At first, I wasn't sure why I attracted it. But then, I figured it out and I can't tell you how excited I am! Okay, I admit, when I first read it I thought the guy just got off the plane from Jerk city. I'll share with you why I'm excited, though, in a minute. First, here is the email. It's exactly as I received it and no changes have been made.

Hi Tony,
Love your article, but just a word of advice: learn how to write. Back

ground is conjugated into one word: background. Did you graduate from college Tony or have any formal education? I know, you're probably thinking, who cares if one can write or has any formal education for that matter. The thing that truly matters in the world of positive-thinking gurus is "empowerment"—why bother with silly things like being educated or knowing how to spell. Or, generally contributing thoughtful public discourse instead of cynically exploiting a growing market of inspirational speaking that is no different than widgets—a system that is neither unique nor revolutionary, just a proven formula of manufacturing a product.

Inspirational speaking is a bankrupt and delusional ideology that neither exists in the real world, nor serves a valuable purpose—merely deceptively oversells the power of positive thinking as solving every problem under the sun, while lining the pockets of snake-oil salesmen like yourself. So, continue to misspell and delude yourself—when you cure cancer instead of peddling pipe dreams to people let me know, I will be truly impressed.
—end—

I'm truly flattered that this person, who did write this anonymously interestingly enough, took time out of his busy day to engage with me his, um *many* philosophies. Notice, it starts out about my spelling but quickly goes into all kinds of fun stuff. There is one phrase that comes to mind that I heard once, *'Dogs don't bark at parked cars.'*

For the record:
- No, I don't have a college education. I thought bankers where more concerned with my financial statements than my degrees.
- No, I'm not a professional writer; however, I figured it was more important to start and get good, rather than wait and do nothing. (Yes, my first six months of posts are atrocious, LOL, but it's great info!)
- I did grow up in a trailer park, actually.
- Yes, I was in a 'death metal' band when I was a teen (It's all over the internet, FYI).
- And yes, I did 'inhale' when I was younger

I did a search on our unkindly friend; it doesn't take a college degree to figure out you can Google someone's email address and find out all kinds of fun stuff about them. I found something interesting. It seems Mr. Positive Pipe Dream Stealer has been doing this for a long time; at least he's consistent! I figure he's extremely wealthy and has a LOT of time on his hands; I bet he's stressed out from working on that cure for cancer too, in between emails, of course.

I posted this because I wanted to share with you that, yes, I get shot at too. It was only a matter of time. Normally, it would be in my network marketing business but now, it's in my blogging, too; it was bound to happen. People like this come into your life and for whatever reason, they feel the need to dump their 'manure' on you, but little do they realize manure fertilizes the soil, even if it stinks to start out with. I could have ignored it, but I felt it served a bigger purpose. I wanted to share it and let you know you're not alone. That's why I realized I got his email. I receive lots of positive emails from people who don't actually post on the blog. I plan on posting them on here, as well. So, Mr. Positive Pipe Dream Stealer, thank you! You've just given me a great idea, even if what you dumped on me did stink. It's exactly what I needed and I appreciate it! :-}

But, this just keeps getting better. Just a few weeks prior, I'd been asking myself what I could do to attract more subscribers to my blog and I applied the five-step method from the book, *The Attractor Factor*. I stated my intentions and then I let it go and let the universe go to work, just like the book states! Lo and behold, a web master that had received my post about Mr. Nasty through the referral of a friend was so impressed with how I turned the negative into a positive that he has now specifically made that post tip #329 in his newsletter to his subscribers; it's now a lesson on how to handle negative clients in a positive way! He emailed me, stating that I should start receiving between five and 75 NEW subscribers to my blog, everyday!

—Anthony Teegarden
www.empower4life05.com
www.empowerment-4-life.com

Anthony's story is an example of the kind of crappy things that can happen to all of us every day; including me. But, instead of letting it affect him, he turned it into something very positive and reaped the rewards. No matter how bad you may feel at any given moment, a great deal of good can come from something that appears to be a humungous pile of manure at first glance.

We live in a world that is driven by beliefs; beliefs about who we are, what we do and what we can accomplish. The law of attraction works by bringing us everything we think about; even those things that are hidden within our subconscious mind. Ho'oponopono is a tool that helps clear away those subconscious ideas that we aren't even aware of and attract all the good things that we want into our lives. Take the example of Debora:

> My father was hospitalized in December of this year and it appeared that he was nearing the end of his very long life. We'd been semi-estranged for many years and I had not seen him for at least ten. Talking to him was always a bit of a trial and although I loved him, I didn't much want to deal with him. I'd been studying a number of things in the months preceding his hospitalization, but the one that was resonating with me the most was *Zero Limits* and I had been practicing Ho'oponopono daily, with a lot more peace in my heart.
>
> My sister had called to inform me it looked like the end, so I decided to call my father. My heart was heavy and I wasn't sure what I could say after all these years, so I did 'I love you, I am sorry, please forgive me and thank you' for a few moments and suddenly, what I might say occurred to me; through inspiration, not memory. So, I called and frankly, I used the mantra itself to apologize for not intending to hurt, but hurting and I asked forgiveness, while also forgiving in my heart and I told him how much I loved him. He didn't say much, but there was a deep softening during the conversation. The next day, he came home from the hospital.
>
> I followed this up by visiting two months after the phone call and the visit was full of love and understanding (of course, I was doing ho'oponopono the whole time I was there). A miracle is what I would call it.

—Debora K. McDermed
www.theverticaldimension.com

I have presented and used many clearing techniques; some of which I wrote about in my book, *The Key*. Ho'oponopono is so powerful because it goes beyond simply clearing the event to real healing of the subconscious mind and taking full responsibility for your own life.

Hitting Bottom

There have been many times in my life when I've struggled with tremendous personal issues. As many of you may know, at one time in my life I was homeless. Not just kind of homeless, as in between apartments, but living on the streets, sleeping in public toilets, homeless. The most interesting thing isn't that I was homeless; it's that it took me years to make peace with the event and clear the negative remnants of that time from my life. You would think that being a self-development guru, I wouldn't have any old issues from the past that still dogged me. But that isn't how it works; for anyone. As I've said, it's like peeling an onion; first you deal with what's on the surface and then you go deeper.

You may find, as I have, that as you go deeper, you also deal with things that may be far in the past. I was homeless as a young man. I'd come to Texas for a job in the oil business about the time oil went bust in the late 1970's. As most people know who live paycheck to paycheck, you're less than a month away from being homeless at any time. Jobs were scarce and I soon found myself with no place to stay, no car and no way to support myself. When I think about it now, I'm amazed by how fast it happened. One minute, I was being terminated along with a group of other men and the next, I was passing a hot check for a couple of burgers, so I could survive.

That feeling of knowing that your life has reached a tremendous low point is crushing. If you've ever seen the movie, *In Pursuit of Happyness* with *Will Smith*, you'll have a pretty clear view of what it's really like. That movie sent chills down my spine and brought back the sights, sounds and even smells of being homeless, like it was yesterday.

When you're in that nightmare, as with many other unfortunate situations, you just focus on surviving and do what you can to block the emotional wreckage that's accumulating in your mind. But in a very short while, the reality can get to you. You stop looking people in the eye and try as hard as possible to make yourself invisible and unnoticeable. People look at you and you feel like a blight on society; a worthless and unproductive lump of flesh that's killing time. This all happened long before I knew anything about clearing or how to turn bad situations into good. The result was that I carried the humiliation and embarrassment of this time in my life around with me for years.

I can say I was in denial. I kept thinking things would eventually work out and they did, but during that time I added to the mental story I had about myself. I gave my state of homelessness meaning and that meaning was that I was undeserving and a failure. It took years; no, decades for me to understand the event and give it different meaning.

Make no mistake, I can't change or recreate the past and neither can you. But I can give it new meaning and allow it to become useful in my life. It wasn't until 1999 that I met Mark Joyner. He encouraged me to share my own tale with people. I was very resistant, at first. Again, the old emotions of shame and humiliation surfaced immediately and I was afraid of what people would think of me. Here again, I was letting the old story I had created of what 'homeless' meant to feed my fear and keep me from moving forward.

I finally did start talking about it and now it's almost like I can't stop. Once I released my emotional attachment to the idea of me being homeless, my creativity really expanded. I also think that my past experience is one reason I'm resistant to quick fix, positive thinking type cures that some people promote. They do a disservice to those who aren't on an upswing already. It makes those people more angry and shameful; I know, I was there once myself. People who find themselves in a pit need a hand up not, pseudo psychobabble advice. That is why I've created *Operation YES*.

When I was homeless I just needed one shot; one little boost and then I could make it on my own. *Operation YES* provides that and stands for:

Your
Economic
Salvation

This is a program of helping people help themselves and the money earned goes to charity. I've always been a big advocate of win/win arrangements and this program is a triple win.
YES wins three ways:

1. People who sign up for the program will get the information they need to change their lives.

2.   The homeless get a hand up through charity.
3.   Those people who help with the project will reap personal and emotional benefits.

Over the past few decades, I never owned who I was as a homeless person, but now I own it. I claim it and have turned it into something positive that helps others, as well. Without question, I have no desire to go back and experience that time in my life, but now I understand the role it played in shaping who I became and what I can do to help others.

In reality, I had the power to let go of that experience all the time, but the story that I told myself stopped me. Stories gathered by you throughout your life limit what you can accomplish. Just think; if I'd continued to deny my experience and hide it from the world, no one would have benefited! Certainly, I couldn't have. I would have continued to harbor these stories in my subconscious and they would have interfered with my forward movement in my own experience.

You may be experiencing some trying times in your own life. No matter the problem or multitude of problems, these techniques can be the first step to real change. Paul relates the following story about his ongoing bout with creditors; a tale many people can relate to, right now.

Ten years ago, I was on the verge of bankruptcy. My mornings began with a wakeup call from the creditors who were kind enough to point out what a loser I was for not being able to pay my bills on time. I wasn't a bad person, nor was I lazy, I just ran into some tough times after taking a few risks on some businesses that I'd started. In those days, I thought the reason I wasn't wealthy was simply because I wasn't involved in the right line of work or the right business opportunity and I blamed circumstances outside of myself, like my bosses or my customers for my failures in life. My world was full of negativity and things were spiraling out of control.

One day something inside me finally snapped and I said, "Enough!" in my head. I had hit my threshold and for the first time in my life, I began to realize that I needed to take full responsibility for everything in my life. Anything and everything that was happening in my life was my responsibility. I was done with being a victim and I was done with blaming the outside world. I realized that opportunities were all around me, but for some hidden reason,

I wasn't capitalizing on them. It had nothing to do with being lazy; it had everything to do with negative conditioning, fear and lack of self understanding.

I began heavily diving into personal development materials and within five years, I was out of debt completely, I was the president and co-owner of a multi-million dollar business, I owned a house and was driving a nice car. However, I was once again finding myself in a frustrated, mental frenzy that was really bothering me. Why? Because my working hours consisted of waking up in the morning at 8am, heading into the office by 9am, working until 5pm, going out for dinner with my wife, heading back to work to work until midnight, heading out for a snack to the local 7/11, going back to work until 2am, then heading home to grab five hours of sleep before I began my work day the following morning. I was pulling 12–16 hour shifts, six days a week, yet somehow after all that work and owning my own business, my income never went past $3,000/month after we paid all our expenses, employee payroll, etc. I was once again frustrated. What else was I supposed to do? I wasn't making progress and there were no more hours in the day left!

Then, my life changed again. Through a series of meaningful coincidences and chance meetings, my heavy personal development track took me in the direction of spirituality and the invisible sides of personal development. I was already great at motivation and taking action and all the visible personal development forces, but I hadn't yet tapped into any of the invisible/spiritual type stuff. I began to attract a series of books and audio programs that I couldn't put down. Instantly, my inner soul knew that this was what had been missing in my life all that time. My income instantly exploded into six figures in less than a year. Books talking about the Law of Attraction, *The Attractor Factor* and the movie *The Secret* started to fill up my shelves.

Since then, I've realized that learning and improving yourself in the invisible world is just as important; if not even more important, than all the personal development we do in the visible world. I learned and became completely clear about the importance of the limitations we impose on ourselves through our invisible limiting beliefs. In late 2006, I enrolled in Joe Vitale's Executive Mentoring program (http://www.joe-vitale-executive-mentoring.com/info.html) and and began to work with a personal coach to really get clear on my purpose and passion in life and start to break down the hidden limiting beliefs that have been secretly hiding deep within my subconscious mind. Clearing these limiting beliefs opened up the floodgates to creativity and I launched my new project called InspiredMoneyMaker.com. I have written several eBooks and continue to write articles aimed to help people all over the world to become inspired money makers and to make money by doing what they love. I feel so blessed to have finally discovered my true calling and to be learning and teaching people to make money by doing what they love.

—Paul Piotrowski
InspiredMoneyMaker.com

Paul points out that loving what you do is a very important part of attracting miracles. Remember when we talked about divine intention and ego intention? This is a good example. Paul wanted to be in business and he was, with limited success. But when he found what he truly loved; what really excited him as his true calling, his creativity and miracle factor increased exponentially.

I know this to be true in my life, as well. My dream for literally my whole life has been to be a writer and I became a writer. I wasn't financially successful for a long time and it wasn't until I found a way for my writing to help others that it really took off. I moved from the ego intention of 'being a writer' and having books published, to a divine intention to help others with what I write. *That* is what excites me each and every day and why I love what I do. You can have all that, too.

There will be times when your life may look absolutely bleak. Simon sent me a story about a series of events that would make a great movie but, unfortunately, he had to live them. You may relate to the desperation he conveys.

Faith has often been defined as a total lack of doubt; that's how you manifest what you need, when you need it. You have to have a total lack of doubt. There's more to it than that, though. You also need to decide precisely what you want, do exactly what the universe tells you to do and of course, never, ever let any doubt creep in.

Ever.

Not all that long ago, I lived downtown and was flat broke. I spent the whole day walking along hot, concrete streets between hot, cement buildings with windows that bounced even more of the early summer heat straight at me, desperately looking for a job; any job. If I hadn't been so broke, I'd have definitely taken public transport instead of walking those hot, city streets and then walking back home again; melting in a suit and tie.

Even when I arrived home, I was greeted with the pile of mail from hell. Employers sent reject after reject: Thanks, but no thanks. You're overqualified, under qualified or we just aren't hiring. There was even a "we're interested. Call us next month." Next month? I need a job now; as in yesterday!

The next letter in the pile wasn't so kind. It said, 'Dear recipient, we're going to disconnect your phone.' Swell. How about an envelope with money; at least enough to pay the phone bill? The last letter wasn't the last hope; it was the last straw, an eviction notice. I had no money for rent, for the phone or for food. Things were beyond desperate.

I recalled that my friend, Lisa, had said that they served free lunches at a day camp and they were looking for some help. I had hesitated because it was about a hundred and twenty miles north of town, but that was all I had taken in about the place; I hadn't been that interested at the time. I was very interested now. I called Lisa, fast, before the phone company cut me off. Yes, there was such a thing as a free lunch, everyday; yes, the camp paid its staff in cash, every Thursday.

Lisa was in a hurry, so she just told me to be on a certain bus at 8:30 the next morning. The bus would take me to the camp so that I could look the place over and maybe apply for a job. She'd fill me in with all the details when she saw me.

The next morning, I'd woken up from one of those dreams you've just got to write down and as I pecked away at the keyboard, the clock ticked on toward the time I was due to be on that bus. In fact, there were three of them, standard yellow school buses, all pulling out onto the road as I zigzagged towards them through a maze of parked cars; late and panting, screaming and shouting for at least one of them to stop for me, please. But not one of them did. With those buses went my hopes for a job and my phone and my apartment. Which wasn't even mine; I was looking after it for a friend. It was his phone bill, too.

I had a pen with me and a plan. I drew PLEASE in big letters on a piece of cardboard and colored those letters in. At the roadside, I held up my sign and stuck out my thumb and assumed I was doing the right thing. It felt right and that was good enough for me.

Nobody who gave me a ride could see any sense in what I was trying to do; get to a camp I didn't know the name of, somewhere a hundred and twenty miles away but precisely where, I had no idea. For me, though, hitching northward was the only logical thing to do. I needed a job at that day camp. I was going to get it. No doubt about it.

So that was why I was feeling slightly stranded and extremely thirsty about seventy miles north of town beside a strangely empty highway. At this time of the weekend, it was usually full of traffic heading north toward cottages in the country or heading south toward the bright lights and nightlife of the city.

But right here, right now, in the throat-baking, dry heat and the blinding sunlight, there was absolutely nothing. No traffic in either direction. There was complete silence, too, except for the wind whistling softly through the grass behind me. Was I still doing the right thing?

Absolutely. No doubt about it. So I waited and waited and waited. Then, I heard a single car engine. It was soft and deep and came from something shimmering shapelessly in the heat haze in the distance.

It was black and white and silver and gold. I held up my sign and stuck out my thumb. There should have been a chauffeur in a uniform and peaked cap; it was that kind of car. It had a black top, white bodywork, chrome pipes along the sides at the front and brass lamp fittings and it rumbled contentedly to a gentle halt right in front of me. The passenger door opened the wrong way round, because the hinges were at the rear and the driver beckoned me in.

"So," he said casually. "Where are you headed?"

"Good question. There's a day camp I need to get to."

"Uh-huh?"

"It's about a hundred and twenty miles north of town."

"Uh-huh."

"I've got to get there, because they're interviewing people for jobs for the summer. Nice car, by the way."

"Thanks. What was that camp called, again?"

"Uh ... I don't know."

"And where did you say it was?"

"I didn't. I don't know that, either."

He took a deep breath. "Oh ... kaaaay ... "

"And they're looking for people and there were buses parked at the shopping mall and I was supposed to be on one but I got there too late and - "

He took one hand off the steering-wheel and held it up to stop me. "No problems—I know the place..."

"You do?"

"Yep. As a matter of fact, that's where I'm headed right now."

"You are?"

"I am indeed; I just happen to own it."

—Simon Carreck
www.thewritestuff.org.uk
www.salespagediagnostics.com

Simon was facing a desperate situation but he didn't sit in his apartment and dread the inevitable, he followed his intuition and stuck to his path and the way became clear. Even in your darkest hour and in the worst circumstances, taking a step in faith will reveal options and possibilities that you would never see otherwise. He got the job and enjoyed it tremendously.

Even if you're not in a dire situation, a miracle can appear that reminds us that the universe is infinitely powerful and our thoughts and intentions, even the ones we make in passing, can manifest in our lives.

Colin lives in Scotland and had planned to fly to Lakeway, Texas for a seminar.

Miracles can happen at the strangest times and in the strangest places. I was 3,000 miles from home, alone in an empty hotel and exhausted when one miracle happened to me.

Twenty-four hours earlier as I packed my bags to fly half-way across the world to attend my first internet marketing seminar, I grabbed a copy of *The Robert Collier Letter Book* to read on the plane. It's a classic book on writing sales letters, written back in 1937 by undoubtedly the best copywriter of all time.

On the plane, after a wonderful meal of smoked salmon salad, followed by filet mignon, I dug *The Robert Collier Letter Book* out of my bag and flicked through the pages. One of the sales letters Collier wrote was for the Harvard Classics; a five-foot bookshelf of classic works of literature. Sitting on the plane, I remembered when I first read this book. I'd thought, "Wouldn't it be cool to get my hands on the original Harvard Classics." Until now, I'd forgotten all about it. Later I slid the book back into my bag, relaxed and watched the snow covered fields of New England pass below.

After a three hour delay at Washington Dulles and a three-and-a-half hour flight to Austin, I arrived long after midnight at Vintage Villas, a small hotel by Lake Travis. In the deserted lobby, I found my room key in a small, antique treasure chest. Up in my room, I dumped my bags and checked out the facilities. I opened a rustic armoire and found the TV. Wedged between the television and the side of the armoire, I noticed three old books. I wriggled them out and looked at their spines.

I was stunned. Standing in a hotel room in Lakeway, Texas, I held in my hands three books from the Harvard Classics collection. The very books I'd read about in *The Robert Collier Letter Book*. The very books I thought would be 'cool' to get my hands on. Now I had.

I learned a lesson that night, standing tired and alone in a strange hotel room in Texas. I didn't need vision boards or a notebook crammed full of scribbled intentions to spark the law of attraction. One simple, magical phrase was all it took; "Wouldn't it be cool..."

—Colin Joss
www.1HourEbook.com

CHAPTER 4

Forgiveness Is Essential

The official definition of forgiveness is to cease to expect retribution for a past perceived injustice and to release the resentment for that injustice. Most of us were raised to know how to give and receive forgiveness from a young age; whether we really meant it or not is another story, but we understood the basic concept. It's a well known fact that anger and resentment that are harbored long term can be physically and emotionally devastating, so it becomes very important to forgive and to do so regularly with everyone in your life.

We all make mistakes and misjudgments and, on occasion, are just plain stupid. I know when I look back at some of things I've done and said (especially as a young man), I can easily forgive others who might not be at their best on a day when I happen to encounter them. But, what about forgiving yourself?

Forgiving yourself is more about not keeping score. I'm sure you know someone who keeps score of every transgression and every deviation from expectation. While you may not be a scorekeeper in relation to others (in fact, you may be very forgiving), it's very common for us to keep score with ourselves. You tally up your mistakes and what you perceive to be your character flaws and revisit them over and over again.

From these past transgressions and negative events that have happened, you develop a story. What does it say about you that your wife left you, your dog died and your truck got repossessed? While it may sound like lyrics to the latest country song, most of us unconsciously keep score like this with ourselves. We decide, based on this assessment, what we're worthy of. Are we worthy of love or wealth or anything better than what we've known previously? We decide and then we put that emotion about ourselves deep within our own minds.

This is the primary cause of so many counter intentions. Our positive thinking conscious self says, "Hey, I can make double my income next year!" While our scorekeeper selves say, "Not so fast. What about that network marketing thing you tried and fell flat on your face? Your life isn't so bad; are you ungrateful or what? Your mom always said it was a sin to be ungrateful." No matter the reason or past negative situation, it's important to forgive yourself and release your anger and resentment, so you can move on.

Not only must you forgive yourself so you can have a better life, your very health may depend upon it. Countless studies have shown that stress and anger can cause or exacerbate diseases such as cancer, heart disease and various auto-immune disorders. When resentment is inter-fering with your life, it's time to forgive yourself. Many people have a constant inner critic voice in their heads, commenting on and evaluating their every move.

Forgiving doesn't mean that you aren't disappointed or upset with yourself on occasion; you're just not taking that to the point of hating yourself. No one can beat you up better than your own inner critic.

One of the problems I see when I talk self forgiveness is that some people think they have to forgive themselves for being human. There are things we can't change as far as the way we look or any disabilities or shortcomings we were born with. These things don't require forgiveness; they just are. You must concentrate on those things that you have done or said that caused pain to yourself or others.

We live in a world with high performance standards and people think they need to be perfect. Yet people do things, intended or not, that hurt others. You may not intend to harm, but the other person is no less hurt. That's when you need to stop at some point and forgive yourself.

Occasionally, people think forgiving yourself means you are letting yourself off the hook and that somehow, the pain and anger you're feeling is your punishment. It also provides an effective barrier to keep from get-ting hurt again.

So, how do you know if you've forgiven yourself and really let it go? The best way to know is if the memory of the event or issue no longer has any emotion attached to it; if you don't feel anger or remorse when it crosses your mind. The release of emotion is key, since emotion attracts things to us so strongly. Once that emotion is released, then you will cease attracting more anger and resentment into your life.

The bottom line is that we all make mistakes and do things we later regret. Forgiveness is like an emotional reset button that allows us to learn and then move on without bringing that negative emotion along for the ride. The following story of Rachel is a good example of what self forgiveness can bring into your life.

As a new bride, kissing my soldier husband good-bye, one week after our wedding left me heart-broken. With tears in his eyes as he boarded the bus he said, "If you can find a way to set us financially free, I'll leave the military and we'll never have to be apart like this again." After years of depression and the humility of bankruptcy, it was hard for me to see that I was deserving of life itself; let alone the abundance of it. But I took him seriously and set aside the emotion from those past experiences. I wanted to be financially free and I wanted my husband back safe at home.

Within two weeks, I found *The Secret*. I stared the universe dead in the eyes and said, "Help me set us free." I got very clear; I wanted to earn $10,000 a month and I wanted to do something I felt passionate about and inspired to do. I wanted to share this secret with the world, but I had no idea how. I followed the guidance from *The Secret* to never worry about the how.

Two weeks later, my father was inspired to tell me about a business opportunity involving the law of attraction. I was ready! Within three months of owning a Law of Attraction *Self-empowerment Home Business*, I made $15,000 in my third month. Yet, our financial troubles weren't over; in order for my husband to leave the military and build our dream home, I would need to manifest $100,000 in three months. A tall order; I felt overwhelmed and a bit stuck. I was then attracted to www.MoneyBeyondBelief.com. The audio on *Emotional Freedom Technique* led me to Joe's book, *Attractor Factor*. Very soon after reading the book and applying the five steps, I cleared my limited thinking. Using these techniques, I easily began to earn $20,000 not monthly, but weekly! One of the most important things I received from *The Attractor Factor* was this question: "Are you focusing on the goals or the spirit that brings them?" Shifting to the spirit instead of the money was the key for me. I never would have believed I could have made over $100,000 in a month and a half with my business! The best part is that by stepping up and allowing more success in my life, I help others do the same. Since I'm in the business of the law of attraction, more money for me means more people are seeing the light, too. What a win-win!

—Rachel Fielding
www.wealthcreatorsunlimited.com

Rachael's experience with past mistakes is common. She could have continued to wallow in the self pity and depression of those mistakes, rather than choosing to release that emotion and move forward. No matter how bad the past may seem, it is just that; the past. It only has the power you give it today and that's your choice.

I like to think of the mistakes I've made as quality feedback along my journey in life. It's much like walking along a gravel path when it's totally dark; you can tell from the feel and sound of the step you just took that it's on the path. When you make a mistake in your life, it's like suddenly stepping into the grass. You know it's the wrong direction and you've been diverted from your true goal or purpose. Rather than focusing on how big a mistake it was or beating yourself up over it, just take another step in the right direction, until you find yourself back on the path again.

Forgiving Past Hurts

Not only is it important to forgive yourself, it's also important to forgive others. You may think that this only really benefits the person being forgiven, but in truth, the one who forgives, benefits the most. Forgiveness has a fabulous healing power on your own mind and heart, even if the offender is long gone or has even passed away.

Don't think for a minute, that I mean you should forgive and forget. It is important to acknowledge past mistakes or missteps in order to prevent them from happening again. But, as with forgiving yourself, it's important to view the circumstances for what they are, or were and release the emotion attached to them as this emotion is what causes mental anguish and brings more similar bad situations into your life. Forgiveness takes us out of the past and allows us to focus on a better today and tomorrow. In effect, it gives you your life back.

I'm sure there have been times that you've been hurt and sometimes, that hurt takes some time to release; I'm no exception. There have been some old, deep wounds that have taken me years to acknowledge and release. You may find this to be true for yourself, as well. As I said earlier, peeling the onion can take years and as you go deeper and work through the layers of your life, forgiveness can offer the healing that you need.

Some people get a little hung up on the idea of forgiveness. I get comments such as, "Well, what if I was horribly abused? Does this mean I have to reconcile with the offender?" Absolutely not. Forgiveness is about you;

not them. You must release your own emotion in order to move on, but that doesn't mean reconciliation. It doesn't matter if the offender even knows you've forgiven them. It matters only that you have come to terms with the incident (or incidents) and refuse to allow it to have any more control over your life.

For deep offenses, it may take years to experience the full freedom of forgiveness. While you may think you have completely forgiven a person or released a particular incident, you will occasionally have those negative emotions resurface. Clearing these emotions is a process, so don't allow yourself to be disappointed if they reappear. It takes time and consistency to clear them from your mind.

No one can force us to forgive and no one can keep us from forgiving. When I've decided to forgive, it often wasn't because the offender asked me to do so or even behaved in a way that created a desire in me to forgive. However, I know that holding onto that resentment could block me from all that could potentially be in store for me and it affects my health and overall well-being. The negativity exhibited every time that incident is remembered lowers your energy and zaps your positive emotions, allowing disease and chronic conditions to manifest and magnify.

True forgiveness brings about a seemingly magical transformation. Whereas we were once burdened, consumed and obsessed, now we're transformed, free and willing. You have taken back control and accepted responsibility. While it might sound harder to assume responsibility for an event or action precipitated by another person, it actually releases you from expecting them to do anything about it. How many times have you gotten irritated at someone when they didn't do what you asked of them? Even something as simple as taking out the trash? The irritation bubbles up within you, doing nothing but damage to your mental state, your health and to the relationship as a whole. Extreme resentment can turn to hate. Hate has the power to create chemical reactions in our bodies. Unresolved hatred and anger have been linked to heart disease, stress and burnout.

If you have an old or deep hurt from the past, it can be difficult to let it go. There are some who don't understand why anyone would hold onto something painful. But, deep wounds can become a part of your identity and they become, in a way, comfortable. It's easy to explain why you aren't moving forward or why you don't have what you want when you have the old, painful, emotional wound to hold onto. People in this situation sometimes can't even imagine who they are, or might be, without their emotional pain. Releasing that pain becomes a journey of not only clearing the emotion, but also a journey of personal growth, as they begin to make room in their lives for positive experiences.

While past events can be painful, you must be able to get to the point of thinking of them without a negative emotional attachment. Know that clinging to the past allows you to feel secure, because it's familiar. Sometimes, we hold onto our past because we are afraid of change and feel insecure about our ability to change. This may provide us a false sense of control or the illusion of control. In reality, the only control you have is to let go. You have no control over the past and can't change it. You have no control over others. You only have control over you and you're the one who chooses to stay in the past; who won't release the past and move on.

Understand that letting go of the past doesn't mean forgetting or denying what happened. Even the traumatic events have shaped the person we have become. Past events are important in respect to how we allow them to affect or guide us in the present. Sometimes, people get stuck in the past and believe that who they were is all they will ever be. To the other extreme, some people decide to rest on past glories and choose not to continue to grow because of past achievements. Both are poor choices, as they prevent continued development.

Be aware that carrying old emotions and baggage from the past can be exhausting and depressing. Think about that when you see someone who seems wrapped up in something that happened in the past. Look at their face and eyes. Do they seem as if they have aged beyond their years? Do they also complain of chronic illness and disease? Many do. Long term, unresolved anger will show itself in your body in one way or another. Staying stuck in the past may cause you to continue unhealthy patterns of behavior that make you feel sick.

There may also be ongoing hurts or individuals that constantly renew these negative feelings. It's important to understand that the only thing you can control is your perception of the situation and that shift in perception is often all it takes to rectify things. Following is Sally's story of just such a situation with her mother-in-law.

My husband and I had been fighting, it seemed nonstop for eight years, about his mother's irritating ways and verbal barbs. I tried repeatedly, without success, to get him to take my side; but he refused! I can't tell you how many times he said to me, "If you can't find a way to get along with my mother, then we might as well just call it quits!"

I knew that I had to take matters into my own hands, as I love my husband dearly and come up with a way to get along with his mother or risk my marriage. I decided to use the teachings of Joe's *The Attractor Factor* and *The Missing Secret* and put all of my attention and focus on positive energy, toward the woman who seemed to be so contrary and cantankerous toward me for so many years.

I started by writing down all the things that I said or did that seemed to upset her over the years and since the incidents bothered me so much as well, it wasn't long before I had documented almost 100 of them! Then, I thought to myself, "How could I turn things around to stop the same old reactions from her and give her what in a perfect world she, and everyone for that matter, truly deserves, which is attention, consideration, understanding and love?" I felt that although she wanted these things, the less that I gave them to her, the more she repelled them. It was an unfortunate cycle and I wanted to turn things around.

Many of the solutions that I put forth on paper I was resistant to, but I decided to try them out as an experiment in humility and compassion. I came up with a rule title and a solution to deal with each and every incident; from household matters, to beauty techniques, to how to deal with that lovely and oh-so appreciated advice on how to deal with my children.

Although these calculatingly affable techniques started out as a tongue-in-cheek coping mechanism, before long I noticed that her reaction to me started to shift; she became more helpful, kindly even and I actually began to like her; a lot, in fact! I thought, if she and I could actually have a non-confrontational, even pleasant rap-port (which has now turned into a loving bond), then maybe these rules really have something to them and maybe I could help to save other young wives years of needless contention by letting them in on my little secret.

I have since published *The Daughter-in-Law Rules: 101 Surefire Ways to Manage (and Make Friends with) Your Mother-in-Law* and am attracting a lot of media attention. I created a new career for myself that brings lots of exciting surprises on a daily basis and gives me a creative endeavor that has led to financial success!

—Sally Shields
TheDILRules.com

Sally's story is a wonderful example of accepting responsibility for what was happening. Did she try to change her mother-in-law? No; she focused on giving her what she most desired. Once you can separate yourself from the irritating and even hurtful events, it allows you to see solutions that didn't even seem possible before. Sally took it a step further. Rather than just improving her relationship with her own mother-in-law, she set out to share this knowledge with others. This is the same motivation I had for creating *Operation Y.E.S.* By turning what was a very bad experience into something that helps others, it attaches a great deal of positive emotion; which attracts those things that you desire most.

As you begin to rebuild your life after getting rid of past hurts that have stood in your way, stay present and aware of what's going on in your body. As the stress lessens and the positive emotions flood in, you will literally breathe easier and your overall health will improve.

Setting out to let go of the past can feel very much like a crisis; it affects every aspect of your present life. Oddly enough, it can produce mood swings as you grapple with the emotions and results of accepting responsibility for your own actions and reactions. It may seem overwhelming, as the ripple effect of positive energy flows through your life. It can feel uncomfortable, like wearing your father's suit or your mother's high heels when you were young. Here again, this feeling stems from the story you are creating in your mind. You are deciding what these new changes mean and what they say about you as a person. Your feelings can range from confusion, doubt and elation to anger or even relief. What happens in your internal world is mirrored by your external world, where your life as you knew it feels turned upside down.

Your comfort zone is the mindset that you've become accustomed to. It is where you feel safe and comfortable. It includes what you believe about yourself and the stories you have created to support those ideas. Anyone who has studied physics knows that it takes much more energy to get an object moving than it does to keep it moving. Once we fall into our personal comfort zone, we cease moving. We get used to our surroundings and actively choose not to leave. We reason that it's better to play it safe than to step out into the great unknown.

Once we understand that risk is natural and to risk intelligently is what we're supposed to do to have a fulfilling life, we can be more consciously aware of the external forces that will hinder us. It takes a shift in our thought process to create enough desire to move beyond the safety of what we have known.

The next barrier to success is the problem of 'knowing versus doing.' Many of us know what to do. We want our time to be our own and to live in freedom. We know we should look for opportunities, take the most promising ones and move forward. If we want different results in our lives, we know we must focus on change. The problem is that we don't change our mindset or let go of the past. We focus on the negative by giving in to fear that we'll fail and it becomes self-fulfilling. It's a conscious decision to accept the mindset of a new and rewarding life and it takes effort. If it were easy, everyone would do it immediately; it took me years!

The power to change any aspect of your life is completely within your control, but only if you change your thoughts. This could also mean changing your associations, but it is necessary if you truly want to live a different and better existence. In order to transform your life and reveal your true self, you must first transform the mind.

Another barrier people often encounter is persistence of action. This is directly linked to the degree of success that you will realize in your own situation. As I mentioned earlier, old habits and thoughts often have to be cleared repeatedly and it's easy to let it go. However, once you do, those miracles that you were experiencing in your life suddenly appear.

Success in any area of change takes work and the amount of work you're willing to put into achieving your dream is directly proportional to the amount of reward you will ultimately experience. One of the greatest issues we face with this barrier is the persistence portion. We may start out strong, but then life gets in the way and we put it off and then put it off again. We start to peel the onion, but then we suddenly stop. Procrastination is not your friend when you're pursuing your dreams.

Procrastination, simply stated, is the passive state of frustration when someone can clearly envision a possibility; a business idea perhaps, a career move or perhaps a relationship change, but all they do is talk about it, think about it, maybe even research it a bit, but then fail to *do* anything concrete to make it a reality.

Step Away from the Potato Chips

One of the most important things you can do to overcome procrastination is to stop daydreaming. A little escape is good for the soul and the imagination is a powerful tool. However, to do nothing other than dream of future success is actually lazy and ultimately leads to a great deal of confusion. It's like that guy who sits on the couch eating potato chips and visualizing his million dollar lifestyle. He then wonders why the Law of Attraction didn't deliver. A healthy mind needs to be focused on actually engaging in life, not just in dreams. Start to employ your imagination into assessing what needs to be done and whether or not your ideas are worth pursuing, then *do it*. The universe loves speed and by acting on your divinely inspired intentions, your life changes instantly.

You can also jump-start your action by setting aside some serious planning time. Focus on your intention and allow the solutions to come to you. Your ideas are not going to organize themselves for you or arrive ready prepared as a successful outcome. You have to do the work. Start to break down what you need to do and make a list of action steps. From your more organized thought processes, you should be able to identify the various steps that need to be taken. Agree with yourself on a period of time to follow the steps and stick to it. Tackle the tasks one by one and identify what you want to achieve at each stage. This will lead to ultimate success.

As you begin to break down your objectives, you will come to realize things that you hadn't thought about during the initial planning stage. This is perfectly okay and you should remain open to modification; just don't use it as an excuse to slip back into procrastination. Be prepared to be flexible about your goals.

A good illustration of this is the story of Peggy and her quest for her dream home.

After I first listened to *The Secret*, I realized I was afraid to really want what I wanted. I decided I really wanted to own my own house. So, I put *The Secret* into action, never doubting that I would succeed.

This was no small feat as I live in Monterey, California; I'm single and only make about $50,000 per year. Most homes cost between $600,000 and $800,000, with mortgage payments double or triple my monthly income. Still, I believed I would and could own my own home and felt as though I already did. After driving around one morning, looking at new homes and seeing myself there, dreaming and visualizing myself in these beautiful homes, I ran to my mailbox, because I decided my mail was good and there was a city flyer that could help me.

Now, normally I would have thrown it away but I decided to read it. There was one sentence in several pages of city happenings that said there would be one home sold in a new development to a moderate income homebuyer. So I had a party, I wrote next to the sentence, "sold to Peggy Sharp" and made cupcakes. I called my friends and planned my move. The following week and only when I felt inspired, I followed up on the flyer and the city planner said, "How did you know?" He wasn't even aware the flyer had gone out. He told me none of the details were together, but eventually it would happen; he also gave me the name of an agency to contact who would screen for the buyer and gave me the name of the person in charge.

I contacted the agency who also said nothing was together yet and it could be awhile and that the home would be advertised to the community, applications taken, a lottery held and a buyer chosen; but nothing was concrete yet. I went on to find out that I was exactly the moderate homebuyer they were looking for, as far as income and every other qualification that was needed. So I cleaned out my closets, had a yard sale and visited the house every day and visualized myself inside.

I found out what the buyer would have to do and in the next few months, I attended a homebuyer's seminar, got preapproved for a loan, cleaned up my credit report and started packing; all before the builder, city and supporting agency even had an agreement. Finally, the home was advertised with a date for application pickup and receipt. I did whatever I was told to do and naturally flowed from the help of one person to another. When I called the mortgage broker, he asked me how I got his number and I couldn't quite remember, just one call had led me to another and another name to another. He said to me, "Well, I guess like attracts like."

The drawing of applications took place, with the rule that the first person drawn would be screened and given 60 days to purchase; if they didn't, the next person in line would get a chance and so on and so on. The night before the drawing, I knew I had a big decision to make, because below market purchase comes with a lot of stipulations, so I had contacted all involved and read over all the rules. Mind you, all these people knew my name by now, because I had called them all several times to keep abreast of things.

When the drawing happened, I was chosen first, out of fifty-eight applicants and I now own my own home in an area where people say it's impossible for someone like me and it's just beautiful.

—Peggy Sharp

The aspect of Peggy's story that I most love is the fact that she set her intention, visualized herself living in her new home and then *did something* about it. She didn't just sit on the couch and hope against hope. She took the steps necessary to make it happen and when it did, she was ready. If she'd waited to see if her name had been drawn, she wouldn't have had time in 60 days to get everything together to get her loan and move!

Just think what would happen if you trusted all your choices and accepted all your decisions; you would be successful in just about everything you do. If you don't trust yourself, you don't trust others. If you don't trust yourself, it shows up in others. In other words, you attract people and situations that you cannot trust. Others accept when you know what you are and do is valuable.

The reason you don't trust in yourself and your power, the reason you don't accept your talents, gifts and abilities like imagination, free will and self love, is because you learned not to trust, not to accept. It's a learned emotion, and once you understand that fact, then you can set about unlearning it. This involves recreating your self-image.

Self-image is how you see yourself in relation to others. It's the story you tell yourself about who you are and what you're capable of. It's very important, as it affects your self-esteem and confidence.

Self-image includes:

- What you think you look like physically
- How your personality comes across
- What kind of person you think you are
- What you think others think of you
- How much you like yourself or think others like you

Self-worth is tied very closely to our self-image. Self-worth can be described as a personal judgment of worthiness that is expressed in the attitudes we hold about ourselves. The picture we hold of ourselves in our own mind is intimately connected to the value we place on ourselves. Healthy self-worth is having a positive constructive view of yourself and your abilities. It allows you to work toward your goals and engage in rewarding relationships. Unhealthy self-worth is displayed as a negative, pessimistic or disapproving view of yourself. It's the inability to see beyond limitations and problems. Those who display this type of worth believe that they can't reach their goals or have meaningful relationships.

Improving your self-image, like improving any skill, takes time and practice. Developing good self-esteem involves encouraging a positive attitude toward yourself and the world around you and appreciating your worth, while at the same time behaving responsibly towards others. Self-esteem isn't self-absorption; it's self-respect.

By working from the inside out and focusing on changing your own way of thinking before changing the circumstances around you, you can build your self-esteem. The goal of clearing away the negative ideas and thoughts is to give yourself a more positive self-image, while seeing yourself honestly and accepting yourself, while removing the internal barriers and self-limiting beliefs that are holding you back.

The biggest mistake you can make is trying to earn worth. As in, "Someday, I'll be worthy." If you spend your life trying to attain worth, you will fail. You must recognize and understand that you have worth and value, no matter what your past or present circumstances are. You are important as a person and can create power from within yourself to accomplish your goals, which are not dependent on what or who you think you are at the present moment. You can create a new you from scratch right now; just because you decide to. You are that powerful.

CHAPTER 5

The Dawn of Awakening

What is it that sets us on the path of self-discovery? Humans have the ability to engage in introspection and choose their own goals, desires and path in life. We can also choose to change that path, as well as our beliefs, at any point. So what precipitates the desire to figure ourselves out? Most people, at some point in their life, realize that the beliefs they have been raised with aren't necessarily what they want for their lives. Some of them may be, but they want to choose. They want to evaluate their beliefs with an objective eye and most of all; they want to choose what to believe and what not to believe.

One of the questions that I'm often asked is, "How can our thoughts be so powerful? They seem to be such fleeting and temporary things; how can they really determine what we do or don't have in our lives?

The mind is incredibly powerful and it is the discovery and direction of this power that can bring you what you desire. It's true that few people will ever stop and think about what creates their thought patterns, feelings and actions. Therefore, most of us have no idea what is responsible for the results we experience in our lives.

Attitude is a composite of your thoughts, feelings and actions; not one of the three, but all of them, working together in combination. These thoughts, feelings, and actions are a product of our conditioned behavior, which includes how we were raised, the education we were given and the people who have influenced our lives. We are all a product of our individual experiences and so, each of us has a unique attitude. In order to understand how these ideas and actions have become ingrained into our behavior, we must understand how we gain them in the first place.

As children, we don't think of ourselves as having choices. We accept what is presented to us by those around us and by the environment. This creates the basis of how we see the world. This is similar to how we learn language. If you were raised by Chinese parents in Beijing, you would probably speak Mandarin and if you were raise by American parents in Connecticut, you would probably speak English. In the same way, if you were raised by entrepreneurs who have limitless thinking, then the idea that you can do anything seems quite natural. However, if you were raised by parents who have always worked for someone else and associate with people in very much the same circumstances, then the idea that you could start a business and make a million dollars would seem very farfetched. We learn these limiting beliefs and accept them as reality throughout our childhood and young adulthood.

As we grow, we roll through life, completely unaware that there are alternate ideas that could benefit us. We don't know what we don't know. Since no one has ever presented the idea that there is something else, we continue along, unaware that we're limiting ourselves.

At some point, we will question our own ideas and beliefs and we may want to change them. It's not uncommon for young adults to test the beliefs they were taught and see if they really hold up. However, most people don't make big changes at this stage. They're just starting out and are searching more for confirmation than contradiction.

How Your Mind Works

You've probably heard numerous gurus talk about our conscious and subconscious mind. This is because they both play a critical role in why we do what we do and they also determine how easily and quickly we can change.

Simply put, the conscious mind is where you receive all the input and experiences from your world. As you are faced with new events and ideas, your conscious mind has the ability to *accept or reject* any idea you choose. When thoughts come to you from your surroundings, the conscious mind is the filter, which allows you to choose only those ideas and events you want to be emotionally involved with. The conscious mind is also where you create the dreams and goals that you want for your life.

Throughout your daily life, you're constantly choosing what your mind will process and be exposed to but, like most people, you probably don't realize it's a choice. This is one of the reasons that the people and circumstance you choose to be around are so important. A negative environment can be very difficult to overcome, while a positive environment gives you an immediate life and enhances your emotional state.

If we're constantly inundated with negative messages, we will choose negative thoughts and ideas, which will be stored in our subconscious mind. We then become a negative person with negative ideas and opinions. The same is true of positive messages. This is because the subconscious accepts what you give it. It doesn't evaluate or calculate; it just accepts.

The subconscious is the 'emotional mind' or 'feeling mind.' The ancient Greeks called it the, 'The heart of hearts.' As we already talked about, it's our emotions that invoke the Law of Attraction and bring to us that which we focus on. If we worry about something happening, then the subconscious will move us in the direction of having that negative thing happen. Likewise, if we create a positive idea of how we want events to go or how we want to handle the unfortunate things that happen in our lives, then the subconscious mind can and will exhibit that positive result. Worrying and focusing on what you don't want takes just as much energy and time, if not more, than focusing on what you do want; it works.

You will always attract more of the same energy that you're in harmony with and if that's negative, then that's what you will receive.

The encouraging message from understanding how the subconscious mind works is that we can monitor our conscious mind and more importantly, we can teach ourselves to increase our positive results. Through repetition of those thoughts, they will become real in our lives.

One way to change negative beliefs you hold about yourself is by changing your thought habits. A thought habit is the self talk you repeatedly engage in. It can be something like, "I'm not a management type, so I couldn't own my own business," or "I'm big boned, so I'll never be slim," or "My folks weren't good with money either, so what do you expect?" You can also have positive thought habits like, "I love myself for who I am," or "Good things will come to me as I expect miracles everyday," or "The Universe loves me!" Do you have a thought habit that confirms a belief about yourself? Is that habit serving you well or is it confirming a belief about yourself that you wish was different?

Results speak louder than words. By choosing and committing to a new habit, you will eventually change your belief about yourself as you create proof based on your results.

It's interesting that many people I talk to think that these ingrained beliefs must have come from a big traumatic experience; actually, the opposite is true. Most develop their beliefs about what they can or can't accomplish from even the smallest events. This is because, as children, these events took on a larger-than-life reality for us. Have you ever revisited a home that you lived in as a child? Were you surprised at how small it now seems, when you remembered it much larger? Now think about an incident that may have happened on the playground or in the classroom when you were embarrassed or made to feel less than intelligent. While in reality the event may have been quite minor, to you it was incredibly traumatic.

Words spoken by a parent or loved one can affect your belief about your potential and your ability to change for the rest of your life, if you allow it. You may have family or friends who constantly tell you to quit dreaming and focus on reality. You have to decide if you will let them limit your life.

Each one of us must remember that it isn't what we're born with or without that determines who we will become. By the same token, you can't blame others for your successes or failures, as that's the road to irresponsibility and helplessness. You can only change yourself and the way you relate to other people. This is the path to true happiness and success.

Knowing that you're in complete and total control of your own destiny, no matter what happens or what others say, gives you the freedom to find your true self and determine who you will become. Following is the story of Peggie and how she overcame the ideas in her own mind to succeed.

In February 2008, I decided I needed to get my act together and decide once and for all what my business focus was going to be. I'd been running a successful pet-care company for nearly five years and was feeling burned out. My heart wasn't in it and it was sucking a lot of my energy away from my passions for healing, coaching and writing. Over the years, I'd had several offers to purchase my business, but still, I was dragging my feet. This resulted in lack. I was mired in place. Watching friends and loved ones head out on the town, while I hadn't paid my mortgage. This sense of lack had me stuck in a place of victimization and fear. Although I knew I was in charge of my destiny, I still felt resentful. I read and re-read Joe Vitale's *The Attractor Factor*. It seemed like nothing happened. I wrote down a number and a date to close on the sale of my business. I created a beautiful vision of being in the place of comfort and having money again. I let go. I knew I needed to clear, so I purchased *The Clearing Audio* (http://www.theclearingaudio. com) listening each morning while writing my morning pages.

Within one day of starting *The Clearing Audio*, I recognized the role I had to play in my success. I finally called the potential new buyer who had written in mid-March. We closed the deal within one week of that phone call. I received the exact amount I had written down in cash, plus $10,000 more in monthly install-ments; all within two days of my 'deadline.' Here's the lesson—I had to take control of my own destiny. It's more than simply writing and visualizing. It's being keenly aware of the tools sent by the universe and then using them!

The Law of Attraction works if you follow the threads from the universe. I'm very grateful to the entire process; as I learned patience, I learned what lack feels like and I learned compassion. Additionally, I learned to initiate what I call active Faith. That's what the Law of Attraction is really about; doing the work. In the past, I assumed that because I wanted things to go easily and effortlessly, it meant that someone would show up with a check and I wouldn't have to do anything at all. Now, I'm clear on the part that my free will plays in every gift I receive. The universe wants me to be happy and will give me every tool that I need to achieve my dreams.

—Peggie Arvidson
http://intuitiveevolution.com

Peggy points out that her feeling of victimization really bogged her down. How many times a day do you hear someone say, "It's not my fault."? How many times have you said it? An incredibly destructive belief that many people hold onto is the 'victim syndrome.' This doesn't mean that you haven't experienced an unfortunate turn of events, but you must remember that it isn't the event that determines the outcome. It's your reaction to that event and your acceptance of responsibility. If you decide to face each difficulty with the attitude of 'poor me,' then that's exactly what you'll get; a poor life. Viewing yourself as a victim of life rather than a participant weakens your resolve and it's very easy to feel trapped and remain the victim for your whole life.

Often, someone caught in the 'poor me' cycle will sound something like this:

- My boss is always undermining me.
- I can't seem to catch a break.
- If there's a loser within twenty miles, I've dated him.
- My wife thinks I'm made of money.
- I can't help it if there just aren't any jobs right now.

The next time you catch yourself exhibiting 'poor me' behavior, try accepting some responsibility by starting every sentence with the pronoun 'I.'

- I choose to stay in my job, although I'm frustrated and unhappy.
- I allow my family to pressure me financially, because I'm afraid to say no.
- I choose to date people that I know I won't like, because I'm afraid of commitment.
- I like people to feel sorry for me, because I have it so hard.

Once you begin to use this technique, you will discover immediately how negative and destructive playing the victim really is. You will also find that you aren't really a victim in most circumstances, except in your own mind. You have the power to change if you want to.

Another destructive behavior that may be limiting your belief in yourself is that of the 'excuse maker.' The excuse maker is incredibly creative when it comes to avoiding or putting off their goals. Many times sounding something like this:

- I'm too tired.
- I don't have enough time.
- I have too many other responsibilities.
- I'm too old.
- I'm too busy.
- I'm too young.

You name it; they make an excuse for it. Many never realize that they've excused themselves right out of living. Alcoholics Anonymous has a saying, "There are a million excuses for picking up a drink; but no good reason."

Have you excused yourself from a college education? From making more money? From finding a great relationship? Excuses abound, but real reasons are few. Take responsibility for yourself and stop making excuses.

This next story illustrates how easy it is to make excuses and how little they really matter in the long run.

I was pregnant with my fifth child and living in a small two bed-room house. I desperately needed a bigger place. There were already four children in one room. My grandpa had since passed away, but when he was alive, he always told me that if I ever needed money to buy a home, just ask and he would help me out. Years had gone by and I'd forgotten about that. My mom suggested that I ask for his help now. Why not, I thought, I have nothing to lose and besides I'd always had a strong belief in angels and the afterlife and I knew that Grandpa wasn't very far away. So, in earnest my prayers began: 'Grandpa could you help me find a really nice place? I need more room and a nice yard preferably; one that's fenced in. A sand box would be nice and maybe a flower garden that I could play in and if it's not too much to ask, a vegetable garden would be sweet too.

I really did put in my order. I was sitting in the tub, actually communicating to him my special request. This was late in May and the baby was due in July. I could feel without a doubt that my Grandpa heard me. Tears streamed down my face and I was sob-bing. I had to stop and just let it go.

The following weekend my husband decided, right out of the blue, that we were cleaning the yard for the day and going to the dump. I didn't question it, but it was odd. Later that afternoon, my girlfriend unexpectedly dropped by and asked us over for a turkey dinner. I gladly accepted the offer. As we were having tea, her brother dropped by unannounced and informed her that he was going to be moving out west; a job transfer and he was putting his home up for sale at the beginning of the week. My radar was turned on. We made arrangements to meet on the Tuesday morning so I could take a look before he listed it. Now at this time, I had no money whatsoever and no savings of any kind; nothing. It seemed a bit silly to even be going to look, but I had to.

On Tuesday morning, I arrived to a beautiful scene, a beau-tiful three-bedroom home, plus an addition with a wood stove. It had a huge white fence all around the yard, with a gate and a nice big shed. Right beside the shed was a big sandbox. All along the walkway was a beautiful flower garden and on the opposite side of the shed was a vegetable garden. I was speechless and sick to my stomach at the same time. I didn't know how we were going to do it, but I had to try. It was everything I had prayed for and more. So I went to the bank, full of confidence (or so it appeared) and told the banker what my needs were and how he could make it happen.

He said, "You have no money."

I said, "I know that. Isn't it your job to find it for me?" Now he was speechless. For every negative, I had a positive.

He said, "You need a down payment of $4000."

"It won't happen," I said, "I don't have that much time." He thought a moment. "Well, if you can get together $2000, I can juggle the paperwork."

"Consider it done," I said.

For the next two months, we ate a lot of pasta and beans and wieners, but nevertheless, I persisted and saved every dime I could get my hands on. A couple of days before closing, I was short about $400. I began to panic. I'd worked so hard and now I was so close. Where would I get the money? That evening, my mother called. It just so happened that she had just received her first unemployment cheque of $454. The bank manager assured me that the funds need only be showing in the account for a couple of days and again, he'd juggle the paperwork. I was in. Just by the skin of my teeth, but I did it.

I'll never forget the well of emotion within me the day the keys were ours. My husband came home and when he put them in my hands, he knew without saying that I had to go and I had to go alone. I went to the house to spend some time alone with my Grandpa and give him thanks for my new home. The baby arrived in July, on schedule and by October, we were nestled in. Some would say that a miracle took place and I really believe it did. They say that sorrow looks back, worry looks around and faith looks up. I just kept the faith. No matter what we want or need, we have to believe it with everything in us and it has to be so.

—Belinda Herbert
Aspiring author and published poet

Not all of us examine our belief systems as young adults. In fact, we can hold off and live blissfully unaware that there is anything amiss; until a catalyst jolts us into questioning who we are and what we really believe. This could be a general dissatisfaction with the life we have; especially if it falls short of our expectations. Or it may be something more traumatic like divorce or the loss of a loved one. A catalyst can be nearly anything that calls into question what we have known to be true most of our lives.

One of the wonderful things about being human is that we all have the ability to change ourselves. Many a person has experienced the glory of a transformational epiphany that has redirected their entire life. They stepped back and recognized the kind of power that exists in each one of us, then set out to harness that power for themselves. You can have this same transformation in your own life, but I will warn you that the reaction from those who know you may come as a bit of a surprise.

Part of your internal dialogue may be that you aren't very smart, that you're not interested in the right things or that the things you do want are out of reach. There's an old saying that "Misery loves company," and so it makes sense that many of the people in your family or peer group may have this same internal dialogue. Unfortunately, when one person in a particular group strives to achieve something beyond what they're all used to, the reaction is negative, rather than positive. We all live in a certain comfort zone and if one of the individuals within that zone steps up to a new level, the others will inevitably try to pull them back. This is an interesting dichotomy unique to humans. We are social creatures and want to belong to a group. However, if that group is holding you back, then you must go forward, even if it means losing some of those connections.

Our group mentality exists mostly out of fear: fear of failure, fear of the unknown, fear of loss. Though the people in your social or family circle may give you negative feedback, they will be convinced they're saving you from disaster. If you examine closely the reactions of these people, you will find that they're not discouraging you due to lack of feeling. They're discouraging you due to their own fears. They wanted you to stay with them, where it's 'safe'.

For many people, this sets up an attitude of helplessness. Some will spend their entire life in this limbo; yearning for a better life but not having the courage to pursue it. They often become bitter and frustrated; have nothing to show for their life but wasted dreams. Time is short and dreams are to be grasped, not heaped onto a pile of regrets.

The first step to getting rid of an attitude of helplessness is to clear your mind of the negative dialogue from your internal programming. As you have a negative thought, stop your mind and clear the thought from your mind. Now, you're free to replace it with a positive one. Negative thoughts build upon one another over time and will crush your spirit. So clearing some, but not others, could lead to bouts of depression and self-pity.

There are three basic categories of destructive dialogue. Chances are you fall into at least one or more of these categories. These categories are Regret, Indecision, and Fear.

Regret

Regret gets everyone on occasion. You may regret unfinished business, shattered relationships or plans that went wrong. Regret haunts people's thoughts, making them hesitant and overly cautious. They are especially destructive because of the story you make about yourself when you start thinking about the 'what if's.'

What if:

- I had taken that promotion?
- I had said yes to that business opportunity?
- I had saved more money when I was young?
- I hadn't given in and made a stupid mistake?
- I'd kept my thoughts to myself?
- I'd finished school?

This type of destructive dialogue only gets worse with time. If you don't learn to get clear and let go of the past, it will keep growing and growing until it overwhelms your present and destroys your future.

Indecision

Indecision is the present reality for many people. Although daily life is full of circumstances that can be interpreted as positive, they respond to their life with a negative attitude. Faced with financial and family demands, for example, they become paralyzed. Afraid of making the wrong decision, they make no decisions and watch their life spin out of control. This negative dialogue sounds something like this:

• My boss has overloaded me with projects. Where do I turn?
• I'm drowning in debt and can't make my payments. What can I do?
• I've just lost my job. What do I tell my family?
• I just graduated with loads of debt and no job. What now?

The main weapon you have for dealing with indecision is focused intention. Focus on the solutions. Take out a piece of paper and write down every possible option or solution you can think of. Then, ask family and friends to add any options they know of. By allowing yourself to explore all the possibilities, you're moving forward. You'll be able to find better and faster solutions by performing this exercise than you would if you just sat and worried about them. The key to dealing with the everyday stress of life is to force yourself forward; even if indecision tugs at you.

Fear

This is a big one for most people. Fear's biggest weapon is the power of 'what if.' It convinces people that the worst is just over the horizon and they should watch out for falling pieces of sky and flying farm animals. This destructive dialogue usually focuses on possible problems, rather than opportunities.

What will I do if the following should happen?

• I get fired?
• I get sick?
• I can't pay my bills?
• I can't find a spouse?
• My spouse divorces me?
• Terrorists invade our country?
• The stock market crashes?
• I lose everything?

I'll be the first to admit that planning for your future is a good thing. However, there's a difference between planning and relentlessly obsessing.

If you fixate on a problem, you've attached a great deal of negative emotion to it and will attract more problems. However, if you look to the future for solutions, you're taking some portion of control over your life; which will free you to receive the miracles waiting to come into your life.

Holly's story is interesting to me, in that she didn't focus on the current situation. Instead, she focused her intention on what she wanted.

I've known for my entire life (I'm 41) that I create my own destiny. I was adopted when I was three-years-old to a family in New Jersey. As a child of three, my teeth were completely rotten from the poor diet supplied by my original family. I had almost all of my baby teeth pulled and finally my grown up teeth arrived, crooked and with an extra fang. I really needed braces, but my mom couldn't afford them. When I was 21-years-old with a full-time job, I decided that I was going to get braces and get my teeth straightened.

After the braces were in place, I asked the Orthodontist, "How long until the braces come off?"

"Unfortunately," he said, "At your age and the amount of work that needs to be done, you're looking at four to five years."

I said, "That's totally unacceptable; these braces will be off my teeth one year from today."

After he stopped laughing hysterically, he said, "No, I'm sorry; that won't happen."

I had to make monthly payments to pay for the braces, so I bet him my last payment (one year later) that the braces would be off my teeth in a year. He was so sure that it wouldn't happen that he agreed; the payments were about $300 a month.

I literally talked to my teeth daily and I went for weekly tightenings. One year to the week later, I entered the doctor's office and said, "Okay, take them off."

I sat in the chair, opened my mouth and he said, "I can't believe it; they're ready to come off!"

"How did you do that?" Unfortunately, I couldn't explain to him how I did it, but I had known I could! I know without a doubt I can create anything; my only problem is deciding what!

—Holly K. Hopewell

Holly could easily have held onto the idea that her original family ruined her teeth or she could have been upset that her mother didn't have the means to get her braces. Instead, she chose to accept responsibility and focus her intention on what she wanted and she attracted that into her life.

Why would you choose to live in constant fear; raining on other people's parades? Why wouldn't you choose to live an abundant and prosperous life? There are many possibilities, but most causes stem from experiences and events in your life. Let's look at a few possibilities.

Conflict with a family member or co-worker can leave you with an attitude of resentment and anger. Do you feel that anger resurface every time you see this person? Do you lie awake at night thinking about the conflict? Do you wish the person harm? If so, then you haven't let go of the conflict. This hurts you more than anyone else and can poison your current relationships.

Do you avoid taking on new responsibilities so you won't risk failure? Do you put others down, rather than congratulate their accomplishments? Do you refuse to assist co-workers for fear they may be after your job? If you find yourself dealing with these feelings, they may stem from low self-esteem. You just don't believe in yourself or your abilities. Individuals with low self-esteem usually try to protect what they have, rather than believing they can have more. The problem is that these negative actions actually have the opposite effect. By refusing to help others and move forward, you attract stress and financial difficulties into your life.

Fear is a natural emotion that protects us from danger. The problem is that many people imagine danger that doesn't exist or is minimal and they magnify that fear until it is larger-than-life. This can be paralyzing; a person living in fear will refuse to consider doing anything outside of their perception of what's possible. They would rather not try at all than have something bad happen; like embarrassment or failure. These people also project their own fears onto those around them, encircling everyone they know with negative energy. They can't handle any type of change without feeling threatened or having an overall sense of impending doom.

Stress is a major factor in most people's lives. Everyone feels financially and emotionally stressed on occasion and no one is immune. The problem comes when that stress is allowed to build day after day, week after week, until it affects every part of your life. Stress will make you short tempered, give you stomach problems, interfere with your ability to sleep and may even lead to thoughts of suicide, just to escape the relent-less pressure. Stress can give you a very negative attitude for a few days, or for years. Alleviating the stress in your life takes effort. After all, it didn't build up overnight and it can take days or weeks to figure out how to lessen the pressure.

There are times when we receive devastating news. But, you must remember that it isn't the news itself that's the problem; it's your reaction to it. Following is Gary's story, which proves this idea.

In the fall of 1988, while shoveling the first snow of the season, I felt a sharp pain in my right hand. Over the next few hours, my right, then my left side went numb from head to toe and my coordination was a little off. I went to my doctor the next morning and he scheduled an MRI as soon as possible. It was Thanksgiving weekend, but they worked me in. On the Sunday evening, the neurologist called my home and wanted me and my wife to come to his office, first thing Monday morning. He also told me he thought they had ruled out a brain tumor. It was the longest night of my life. I had two young sons and I wanted to see them grow up.

The next morning, the doctor took over an hour telling my wife and me everything that wasn't wrong with me. He finally said I had three choices for what was wrong: MS, MS, or MS. He told me to prepare myself for death or a wheelchair within ten years. I told the doctor that the diagnosis was his opinion and that I wasn't going to wait for it to catch me.

I knew I needed to create a vivid visualization of what I wanted my future to look like. First, I created my 100th birthday party where I would jump from an airplane to celebrate. Next, I had to change my current physical state. I found out just enough about MS to know that for some reason the myelin sheath that covers the nerves dissolves. The exposed nerves then touch and short out, creating a blockage to whatever area of the body that nerve served. You can lose feeling, coordination, sight, hearing, even life.

I didn't like the sound of those options, so I set out to create my own reality. I wanted a visualization process that directly countered what MS does. Since the myelin dissolves, I decided to create an army of beavers to go to work in my head to patch up the nerves. I would spend two to three hours a day seeing the beavers going all through my brain, patching up all the exposed nerves. I had foremen and skilled workmen, a payroll office and a store for supplies. There were three shifts working around the clock because money was no object; I was worth it.

Though I shared my vision with my doctor, he told me not to expect too much from what I was doing. I decided to stop seeing him, as he was too resigned to 'my fate.' My symptoms improved and I continued with life. About five years later, I applied for an insurance policy and they required another MRI. The new test showed that 90% of the previous scar tissue was gone. The new neurologist said that wasn't supposed to happen and I still had MS. I have never owned the illness by saying I had it; period.

This coming Thanksgiving will mark the 20th year since my first diagnosis. In the last 20 years, I have completed a 40-foot fire walk, bungee-jumped, trapezed, climbed 14,000-foot mountains and played the drums in a band. I'm currently in flight school, among other things. I see this experience as one of the greatest blessings I could have been given. My attitude is that I have two choices about my life: GOOD and GREAT. With those options, I might as well choose GREAT!

—Gary Barnes
www.maxlifeinternational.com

CHAPTER 6

The Attitude of Gratitude

Living with an attitude of gratitude can make all the difference in the world. If we lose sight of it, we can give up our focus and our purpose. To do the things I love to do and help others find their full potential is my purpose. Every morning, I sit on the edge of my bed and say out loud, "I am so grateful for this day."

Everyday that we wake up is another blessing. I'm thankful for those things I see and have, but also for things that are coming to me in my life. You will release the toxins in your system with this kind of attitude. If you harbor resentment, it builds up inside you. You're the one who pays the biggest price, not the person you're upset with. They may not even be aware of your resentment or they may choose to ignore it.

Dwelling on circumstances that aren't going your way builds negative energy. It adds toxins to your mind, heart, and body. The obstacle that stops you from becoming the person you want to be and having what you want grows from negativity. Learn to be thankful in all things. You don't have to remain stuck in your discomfort or pain. Begin by being grateful for little things.

If you find yourself in a thought pattern that keeps pulling you down into that old black place, think of one small thing you're glad to have. It might start with, "I'm thankful for a cup of coffee this morning," or, "I'm glad the sun came up again." Then say out loud to yourself anything that comes to mind for which you're grateful.

You don't like your boss? Be thankful for your job and for the possibilities in your future of a better job. Talk about your future with your mentor, friends and family. It's not the someday that so many people talk about. You can visualize yourself taking an interview and being hired for the job you truly want.

Gratitude is the recognition of your gifts. Again, it is a verb, not just a noun and requires action from us. The seed of your actions begin with your thoughts. You can ask for and attract good things into your life.

I hear individuals constantly say, "It's easy for you to be grateful, you have everything and I have nothing!" All I can say is that it didn't start that way and if I hadn't learned to be grateful when I had very little, then I'd have no idea how to be truly grateful now. I call this the 'I'll Be Grateful When' Syndrome. Many people think that when their life turns around and goes well, then they'll be grateful. They don't realize that the fact that they're not grateful now is inhibiting their ability to gain what they really want. This is because they're missing the positive emotional energy that gratitude brings and so, they miss what they could be attracting.

I tell everyone to find something, anything, to be grateful for. When I was first introduced to the idea of this type of gratitude, I really had nothing. I was a struggling writer with more creditors than friends and I couldn't quite seem to ever get even; let alone ahead. One day, I was writing down some thoughts on this idea of gratitude and trying my hardest to find something to be really grateful for. I thought about it awhile, then stared out the window and thought some more; still nothing. I twirled the pencil in my hand trying to think. I stared at the company logo and the #2 imprinted on the side of my yellow pencil and it finally hit me; I'm thankful for my pencil! I realize it may sound a little silly, but I focused on the idea that my pencil gave me the ability to capture my thoughts on paper. It also had an eraser, in case I wanted to refine those thoughts into something better. While it wasn't much; it was something.

You have to find something in your life to be grateful for. Perhaps it's your pet, or a close friend. There's always something. One of the biggest challenges in being thankful is the energy we carry in the old internal dialogue we carry with us. We forget that all the experiences in our past, positive and negative, make us who we are today and we can now choose to accept them as all positive and make something good from them. One of my favorite affirmations is to say, "This is the greatest day ever, because my feet are above ground and I'm alive and well."

The more I studied gratitude and how it could affect my future, the more I was amazed by it. I found out that gratitude lies within all of us and is a choice not dependent on circumstance. It can also be developed by everyone. If you've experienced difficult times in your past, you can still become a grateful person.

The person who looks back on their life and sees things in a positive way will see his future as one of satisfaction and success. It all starts and ends with the attitude of gratitude we are talking about. This gratitude is one of the quickest ways I've found to start the law of attraction working in my life.

The concept of gratitude doesn't mean I have to be happy in every circumstance. It doesn't mean staying in whatever your situation is and finding something to be glad about. Some people might think that this new attitude can make you passive and somehow content, no matter what your circumstances. That isn't what I'm trying to say. If your surroundings and your friends need to be changed for you to have a better life, then by all means, do what you need to. I did and you can, too; with the help of others to support you.

As I learn and experience more in being able to help people, I realize that I've been given many possibilities. I'm the one that needs to decide to take the action needed and move forward. I realize that it's a choice to have gratitude as one of the main focuses in my life. When we go through difficult times, we can learn to be thankful that we have the strength to get through them. It helps us to get over things and move on. It is helpful to remember that hard times are only temporary. The good thing about being grateful when things are going well is that it helps us to enjoy it all the more.

Scientific and medical researchers agree that the well-being and health of a person relates to gratitude and the role it plays in their lives. It is appealing to our emotions and encourages us to be kind to each other; gratitude makes us feel more loved. We are more likely to do kind things for others and receive the same treatment. Expressing gratitude also makes us feel more alert, enthusiastic, optimistic and energetic. With gratitude, you will make progress toward reaching your goal of abundance.

Gratitude Alters Your Perspective

If your attitude is one of gratitude, you are always thankful for something. That creates positive energy and helps you attract abundance now and in the future; no matter what your past has been like.

If we depend on others or blame them for our attitudes or moods, we give up our own power to create things from within our spirit. Other people are going to act however they want to, but we don't have to be controlled by them. We can decide to have a grateful attitude about things; no matter what.

I've learned over the years that life is partly what happens to me and mostly how I react to what happens. Instead of it making me feel bad or angry, I can react to it in any way I choose. I can look in the experience for the lesson or the blessing and be thankful. You're in charge of what your attitude is, everyday. It's not anybody else's fault. Don't let other people tell you how to feel or how to act. Develop the attitude of gratitude and it will be a blessing for you. You will have a more abundant life.

If you have gratitude in your daily life, you will be much happier. You can walk around feeling miserable, or you can be happy and a stronger person. It takes as much effort to be miserable, so why not just choose to be thankful?

You may think it sounds strange to say that the work is the same for both attitudes. Look at this way: you use the same amount of energy to say something nice as you would to say something negative.

This change in the way you think is not automatic. It will take some effort on your part, but it will be well worth it. Like playing a sport or a musical instrument, the more you practice, the better you become. It will unlock potential inside of you that you may not be aware of, yet.

To move forward in your path, you need to move from thoughts to words, on to feelings and finally, actions. When you're moving forward, it is with a positive and thankful attitude that starts in your mind and in your spirit. You look for how to accomplish something you want, rather than being stuck with negative thoughts. You don't just sit around, telling yourself that what you want can't happen. It can be done and you know it. There are steps to get what you want. Gratitude for what you have and for what you're bringing into your life are important parts of that process.

It's all about deciding to have a positive and grateful attitude. You can bring it into your life and share it with others. It's not about the negative experiences or things that life has brought to you in the past. It's your state of mind. Your mind decides on the attitude you bring to everything.

The more thankful you learn to be; the easier it will be to see things you can be grateful for. It really is your mindset. It gives you a way of looking at things with new eyes and a new perspective. It's easier to see things more clearly from the past if we get rid of old, negative energy. Then we can look at it with gratitude.

The attitude of gratitude will make a big change in how you feel when you get up in the morning and when you go to bed at night. People around you and friends will ask what's different about you. What's going on? You're a different person. You're so much better off than you used to be. It's within your reach to develop and use gratitude in your everyday life.

The most powerful way to use the Law of Attraction is to be grateful. Gratitude is the best way to change your level of vibration. Gratitude should be expressed in every aspect of your life. Don't take life for granted; you will be depleted of energy and in the end, you'll have sabotaged yourself. Expecting miracles without gratitude for the things you have may cause anger and resentment. The practice of gratitude allows you to tap into the unlimited energy reserves of the universe.

I'd been on the waiting list of a service dog organization for two years. I'd been told that was the estimated time that I'd have to wait for a dog to become available. At the end of those two years, I found that there would be an additional two years of waiting, as there weren't enough trained service dogs for the number of applicants.

I wanted and needed a companion dog in my life! I decided to take action. That weekend, I made a list of what I wanted in a dog. I stated my preference to be a female Golden Retriever. On Sunday night, I made my call to the universe for my service dog.

On Monday, I was led to call the animal shelters and veterinary offices in my area. I gave them my list of requirements for a dog that would be owner-trained as my service dog. I asked that if any possible candidates came to their attention, would they please call me.

One week later, I received a call from one of the animal shelters that I had contacted. They felt they had the perfect dog for my needs. The dog had been turned in to the shelter on the same day that I had called in my request. She had been found running loose in the desert, 40 miles from any habitation. The week-long delay was due to the legalities required to make dog adoptions legal.

I went down and met my new companion. Amber came right up to my wheelchair and sat next to me. We walked about the lobby as if we'd been working together for years. Amber exited the shelter and rode the lift up into my van as if she'd been doing it since she was a pup. The look she presented to the world from that lift, while rising into the air, was so royal that my new companion was ever after known as, 'Amber, the Princess of the World.'

I was blessed for ten years with Amber, my companion from the universe. My wish for others is to 'have the faith' and know that only the best can be our gifts to ourselves when we let a higher power provide for us.

—Teri Dykes

As a child, you were taught to say thank you; thank you for a drink, a piece of chocolate or a gift. For many of you, forgetting to say thank you meant trouble. This practice of gratitude stayed with you as an adult. As an adult, your gratitude turns toward things like:

- A home.
- Your family.
- Your friends.
- Your job.
- Your material possessions.

Your gratitude is focused on your present circumstances and your material possessions. You've been conditioned for this type of gratitude since you were a child; to automatically say thank you before you really had time to realize what you had. True, it's better to be grateful than not, but this form of gratitude is ineffective in activating the Law of Attraction. More often than not, when you practice this form of gratitude, you're just looking at the glass half full. You're just going through the motions of accepting your circumstances. You make statements such as:

- "At least, I have a place to live."
- "I'm just grateful to have a job."
- "It's not much; but it will do."

Read these statements aloud and really listen to them. They sound much more negative than positive. They have an underlying message of, "I'm not really happy with what I have in life." People who make statements like these aren't excited about their life. They feel empty on the inside; they're just going through the day-to-day motions of life, not truly appreciating what the world has to offer. They're actually expressing complacency, rather than gratitude.

Ineffective gratitude is not strong enough to activate the Law of Attraction. It's just a quick fix for a bigger problem. After a few days, you're back in your old frame of mind. The first sign of adversity takes you right back to the 'at least' mindset.

Effective gratitude, on the other hand, is a deeper understanding that leads to tremendous prosperity. With effective gratitude, you are still thankful for your material possessions, but you now have a greater appreciation for:

- All of your life.
- All of your thoughts.
- Your emotional state.
- Your problems and trials in life.
- Your conscious awareness.
- Anyone who is unkind to you.
- Any mistake you make.

You may have read this and said to yourself, "Why would I be grateful for anyone who was unkind to me?" or, "How can I be grateful for my problems?" Well, the answer is simple. You're grateful just to be in existence in the universe. Your circumstances don't matter; all that matters is that you exist and you're here for a reason.

You become grateful for all aspects of your life; every up and down, every trial and tribulation. Everything in your life is a learning experience that will lead you down a path to prosperity and abundance. You are grateful for every opportunity, no matter how good or bad, the universe sends your way. Gratitude paves the road on which your life travels.

This may seem difficult to understand, so let me give you a mountain climbing analogy. Imagine yourself climbing a mountain. You're in awe of its beauty. You are so fascinated by its mystique that the level of difficulty to climb it is the furthest thing from your mind. It doesn't matter how dangerous it is to climb; all that matters is the experience. If you can remain in that frame of mind, you will scale that mountain without one ounce of fear. Soon, you will have stood atop many more mountains, reveling in your life's experiences. Gratitude is a powerful tool that will help you overcome any obstacle in life.

Effective gratitude equals prosperity. True prosperity is impossible without true gratitude. So, in order to increase your prosperity, you must focus on the deeper side of gratitude. The more grateful you are, the more prosperity you will experience, thereby attracting more abundance into your life. For this reason, the practice of gratitude goes hand-in-hand with the Law of Attraction.

Ridding your mind of ineffective gratitude is imperative to experiencing effective gratitude. Once you have mastered effective gratitude, you will shift to a state of grateful existence. At this level of gratitude, you can activate the Law of Attraction. Your gratitude is vibrating throughout the universe. It's impossible to separate yourself from gratitude and as a result, you begin to attract the circumstances that resonate with who you are and what you desire.

This situation is exactly what happened to Cesar.

In 2001, I had the privilege of translating Joe Vitale's *Spiritual Marketing* (which was the precursor to Joe's more updated book, *The Attractor Factor*) into Spanish. I didn't realize at the time that I was going to have the chance to test the principles in that book to such an extent. Sure, I had attracted many small things from new friends, to extra money, to new business contacts, but nothing to the extent of what I was about to manifest.

My wife and I have a timeshare property near Cabo San Lucas, Mexico. During one of our visits there, we met with some local Lions Club members; I belong to the Santa Ana Lions Club. During one of our many pleasant conversations, they asked us if we knew of a way to get a fire truck donated from the United States. They had heard that it was possible because another fire department had done it in the past. The fire truck they had at the time dated from the 1950s and it was getting pretty expensive just to keep it in service.

I told them I would see what I could do and when I came back home, I started looking around at the different options. In the meantime, I was visualizing the actual delivery of the fire truck. Then, I let it go.

Suddenly, I found out that a local auction had a fire truck in inventory. I had some extra money that I'd attracted, so I set a limit of what I could pay for this fire truck: $3,000. As you know, an auction can get out of your budget pretty quickly and these were cash only transactions.

When the time came to begin the auction for the fire truck, the auctioneer said, "I'll start the bidding at $10,000!"

TEN THOUSAND DOLLARS!?!?! My heart sank as I heard that number. So close, but yet so far. Had all that visualizing not worked? Had I forgotten to clear something?

As I was pondering these questions, I realized that there was no response from the hundreds of people who were there with their bidding paddles. They were there for the sports cars and the 4X4 trucks, the Mercedes and the Jaguars. I had a different intention.

Then, the auctioneer started lowering the starting bid amount. "I'll take $8,000."

No response.

"Seven thousand dollars." Silence.

"$6,000... $5,000." Suddenly, he blurted: "I'll take ONE THOUSAND DOLLARS"

My hand immediately sprang up toward the sky, carrying with it my bidding paddle. Then the auctioneer began his job and asked for $1,500. Someone responded.

The bid was called for $2,000. I bid. Then, it started going up in $100 dollar increments. I finally stopped at $2,500. The other person thought better of it and didn't bid; neither did anyone else. The fire truck was mine for just under $3,000; including all the fees and taxes.

The following Monday, I found a friend who could help me pick it up, because of course, it's a big truck and it requires a different license type to drive it in California. Later that week, I was able to attract a person who knew someone from the local fire department, to give the fire truck a clean bill of health for operation. Everything was in perfect working order.

Now that fire truck is at the Cabo San Lucas Fire Department, right on the main boulevard, behind the McDonald's; all made possible by the principles in *Spiritual Marketing*, thanks to the Law of Attraction.

—Cesar Vargas
www.mercadotecniaespiritual.com

Gratitude isn't automatic. It's not something you were born with. You have to teach yourself to acknowledge the prosperity in your life; no matter how small or large. Your thought process has to be transformed from expectations to gratefulness. Always practice gratitude despite any negative circumstances surrounding you. You can't waste your days dwelling on what you don't have and what's missing from your life. Instead, focus on the prosperity and happiness in your life and that is what you will receive. The following are a few suggestions on how to express gratitude:

- Turn gratitude into a habit. Ingratitude seems to be a trend in today's society, so this may be uncomfortable at first. Stick with it; in the end it will be very much worth the effort. Saying thank you takes only minutes of your time, yet makes a tremendous impact on the universe. Soon you'll find gratitude is addictive.

- Practice, practice, practice. Say thank you repeatedly. This acknowledges the gifts of the universe. Don't take your prosperity in life for granted by not saying thank you. Thank everyone in your life - parents, spouse, children, salesmen, co-workers. Anyone who may have given you even the smallest amount of abundance in your life; be grateful to them. You never know. By telling them thank you, you may have inadvertently taught them to be more grateful in their own lives.

- Give back to the universe on a daily basis. You don't have to write a large check to a charity; you can instead offer to carry someone's groceries to their car for them. Pick up a piece of litter and throw it away. Let someone in front of you in traffic. The vibrational energy is the same for any size of gratitude.

- Turn your practice into a ritual. Develop your own personal rituals. Count your blessings each day. Say thank you for the beautiful nature around you. Say a small word of thanks before a meal. This will help the prosperity to flow into your life without limits.

- Write down all of your abundance. Whenever it is convenient for you - morning, afternoon, or evening—write down every fantastic thing that has happened to you. This allows you to acknowledge the positives in your life and remove any negative thoughts or feelings. Write everything down, no matter how small you think it is. "I'm thankful my car started this morning," "I'm thankful that I'm able to work with such nice people," "I'm thankful that I'm able to enjoy the beautiful park next to my office." Your life is a gift and you should be grateful for each moment.

- Take some time away by yourself to enjoy an activity that gives you pleasure. It can be aerobics, jogging, dancing, reading or any other relaxing pastime. This can soothe you and shift your perspective to a more positive one.

- Stop and be grateful. Take time during your day to relish in all that you have to be grateful for. Meditation, prayer and spiritual reflection are important tools that you can use to reconnect with the universe and realize that you are part of something much larger than yourself.

- Set gratitude reminders all around you. These can be anything from inspirational quotes, a card from a loved one or a picture of an awe-inspiring natural landscape.

After getting laid off for the second time in a year, I recently decided to just jump into building my own business; but I was scared to death. My mind was giving me a million reasons not to and my body was racked with terror at the thought of failing. Please note that I did this at a time when I didn't know how I was going to pay the next month's rent. All my past fears of failure and all the memories of loss, lack and poverty were returning to taunt me.

I've been a student of Joe Vitale's for almost three years and I've integrated many of his practices into my own tapestry. I used *The Secret* as a starting ground to remind me of the shift. However, I also watched the *Subliminal Manifestation* movie (http://subliminalmanifestation.com) over and over again. I knew that if I held my fears in front of me and focused on them, I wouldn't get very far; other than deeper into my fear. My clear aim was to succeed and move beyond 'surviving my life' to living my life with all my being.

So I made a new decision. I decided that my business, *Transformational Resources* was successful and abundant. I decided that it was easy to get clients and that money was flowing easily in and out of my life. The first thing I did was to stop being angry with the people who laid me off and I did the forgiveness blessing ritual with them. I felt my body relax, my mind let go of running the picture again and again of each scenario and I knew I was at peace. From there, it was time to create!

Then, I got excited about what was next! My past way of doing things involved me always looking for 'what's wrong or what going to go wrong?' in any given situation. In getting excited, I've been able to see the wonderful things and people in my life. I started writing and opening myself up to connecting with people, through my own blogs. I love to write and I realized that it was time to stop withholding a gift I've been bestowed with.

On a deep inner level, I've begun to see how I can be of service to the universe. Three times in as many weeks, someone has gently reminded me that the real key is to ask not what can I gain from something, but to ask how can I serve? With a name like *Transformational Resources*, my vision is big and evolving. This slight, albeit not so subtle, shift in mindset alone has me looking at every possible event I plan as an opportunity to be of service, rather than a way to make a lot of money. I let go of the energetic attachment to the dollars, just as Joe described about the gold lighter. It's been absolutely amazing. I still giggle every time I win a project.

Within 2 weeks of really embracing these decisions, my phone has begun to ring off the hook, my pipeline is filling up and I'm meeting more and more people 'as if by magic' who connect with me in divine perfection. These connections are gems. I'm actually working now with someone who will have events during the Democratic National Convention in Denver in August, 2008 and through her; I've met with some of the top staff in the Host Committee. All because I took a chance!

In case that wasn't enough confirmation that what I was doing was working, I met a woman from the local Women's Chamber of Commerce through a series of divine synchronicities who invited me to a big event at INVESCO Field. While I was there, I saw a past client from the job where I was laid off. Through the course of our conversation, he asked if he could write a letter of recommendation. Being that this is a local non-profit organization and it was a huge event that I planned for them, I gladly accepted his offer. When I read the letter today, I cried. This letter was the most amazing and humbling reference I've ever received. I am so grateful for this and all the blessings in my life. This has not been an easy process, but it most certainly has been one of the biggest periods of growth in my life.

This decision was a huge step for a single mom and the amazing thing is, at 41 years-old, I've just begun. I've done some incredible things in my life and I look forward to manifesting miracles in my life and the lives of others.

—Suzan Patrick
www.transformational-resources.com

CHAPTER 7

A Miracle a Day

The best thing about having miracles coaches is all the fabulous stories I hear from people just like you. These are ordinary individuals who have learned to harness the power of the law of attraction and expect miracles in their lives.

Attracting London and Paris

I love to travel. Last year, I discovered home exchanges. Chris, my boyfriend, and I were planning our annual four-to-six-week vacation adventure. We didn't know where yet. We had to leave in only thirty days and I was waiting for inspiration. This was it. I joined two home exchange websites and started to contact people in London and Paris.

As I emailed people in the home exchange system, I began to imagine what it would be like to visit the places I'd grown up in with Chris. I was unsure we would get any exchanges at all with such short notice. Indeed, all of the responses I got said, "Thank you, but we've already arranged an exchange".

I decided to use my experience and understanding of deliberate creation to create what I wanted. I let go of the 'what if's' and the feeling of desperate hoping and just 'saw' and believed it would happen. I had *The Attractor Factor* and I combined those steps with my meditation and self-hypnosis experience. I decided I wanted to go to London and Paris.

Within a week or so, we received an invitation from a lady who lived on the outskirts of London! Hooray, it worked! We arranged to exchange homes with her for two weeks, free lodging! I continued to email more people in Paris.

No one took us up on our offer in Paris before we left, so we got our tickets for 28 days and flew to London. We had a great time there, staying in the moment and enjoying what we were experiencing. We drove to Manchester and Scotland with some friends.

Then, when we were in Scotland I received an invitation via email from a couple who lived in Paris. He was originally from San Antonio and so he picked us out of the thousands of listings and asked if we would stay in their Paris apartment for a month and feed their cat and water their plants! They didn't even want to come to our house; they had other plans! Amazing! We were thrilled! My spirit was dancing; I was so thrilled I could create my own reality. It was easy and fun. We rearranged our tickets and spent an absolutely fantastic month in Paris. Having a free, four-bedroom apartment in Paris still seems surreal to people when I tell them about it; I can see the doubt in them. They think, "Well, maybe for you, but that would never happen for me." However, it can happen for anyone. All possibilities are available at all times and we get to choose. Change your thoughts and believe you can and it will appear. Look for it…and be happy!

I was so excited. I knew in my heart it would work, I saw it and I kept the faith. I also didn't let myself be attached to it. I always say, 'this or something better.' This is because often the universe has something even more wonderful than I can conceive of for myself and I want to be open to it. I also recognize the negative energy from fear, disappointment and frustration, which I could have easily fallen into. I could block what I want from coming to me. In fact, I have seen circumstances where what I wanted was right in front of me, but I didn't see or realize it, because I was so caught up in my thoughts and frustration.

I continue to manifest the most amazing home exchanges. I keep the energetic 'invitation' out there and I am open to what new adventures the universe has in store for me. Last year, we had six weeks free, this year our whole trip is 100% free; lodging and free cars, too! This year, I've attracted six new exchanges; Paris again, (of course) Rennes, France, a mansion on the beach in Virginia, Mexico, New Mexico and Spain. I love to travel and this is my dream coming true; new places, people and free places to stay!!

—Nan Akasha
CreateYourOwnRealityNow.com

The Perfect Day

I knew Paris well from my youth, but hadn't been there in 24 years. Chris had never been there, so I let him pick what he wanted to see first. He wanted to go to the Eiffel Tower first, then Notre Dame and then eat in the Latin Quarter; in that order.

Prior to arriving, I began to visualize what it would be like. I saw in my mind's eye Chris and I wandering Paris, laughing, happy, having a great time and meeting wonderful people. It all started with a closed metro line and plans that were completely derailed…thank goodness! We had a divinely guided day, the universe took us to all the right places at all the right moments; it was so magical! We got delayed going to the Eiffel Tower, so instead of going when we planned (about noon), we ended up there just before dusk settled over the city and the lights came up. We got to see the view in daylight, sunset and dark. Beautiful! Then the tower lit up with all these sparkling lights for ten minutes each hour. We saw that from the ground as well as when we were on it!

We also got delayed getting into Notre Dame and ended up arriving as they started a service! It was so unique and special; we wandered around looking at the splendor with incense smoke filling the air, light streaming from the stained glass windows through the smoke and the voice of this amazing woman singing filled the air; it was truly ethereal!

Finally, we were at a loss as to how to get from Notre Dame to the Eiffel Tower, as they closed the underground at the Eiffel Tower. We saw a 'Batobus'; a boat bus which we rode along the Seine and got to see all kinds of sights through the huge glass dome covering it… lovely!

Finally that evening, going home to our free apartment, the train skipped our stop. It was so late that there were no trains going back in the other direction, we had no map of the area and there are no taxis in general that far out of Paris. It took awhile and we arrived home at 2:30am, but visualization and law of attraction stepped in! We tried to find someone, catch a bus; nothing. No one was around, so we tried to call a taxi on our U.S. cell phones. I was on hold with taxi companies for over 30 minutes; in French! They wanted a specific address and a French phone number, of which I had neither. After starting to panic, I stopped, took a deep breath and started visualizing Chris and I getting into a car and arriving back at the apartment with laughs and smiles. Suddenly a taxi, empty and with a light on, appeared from nowhere! We jumped in front of it and although he stopped, he didn't want to unlock the doors. I convinced him, however, when I told him the address, he vehemently refused. He said he was from Paris, he didn't know the area and he wouldn't take us. I was NOT taking no for an answer, I kept breathing and seeing us happily arriving at our apartment in my mind. Somehow I managed to convince him to please try and I would guide him; as if I knew where I was. We picked our way along, I kept telling him go this way, go that way. I was going by total intuition, but we found it! By the time we arrived, the driver was on our side; happy and cheering that we had found our way and wishing us well. He got a big tip and went home happy!

Days like that are treasures. By always putting out to the universe what I want (or something better), the universe opens doors I didn't know existed. Listen to your feelings and you will follow them to a trail of fantastic experiences!

What I have learned from travel is to go with the flow. Things always change and are different than what you expect or plan. The key to enjoying the trip and encountering the wonderful surprises that are out there is to be flexible and open. Make plans, but be open to let them change and adapt as you go. Be aware of what else is going on around you and let the plans slip away if something wonderful appears.

I never could have planned such a wondrous day, timed everything so perfectly and encountered the sights, experiences and people we did by my planning alone. Allowing the universe to take my desires and create the better plan, letting go and enjoying the moment, allowed me to experience what has become one of my most memorable days ever.

—Nan Akasha
CreateYourOwnRealityNow.com

Baby Whispers

The voice on the phone sounded mature and young, strong and tentative, all at the same time. When I mentioned that I'd just come from a voice lesson, after hearing that she was a singer, she seemed pleased. Both of us were a little nervous, but that feeling seemed to lift almost immediately. I felt familiar and comfortable with her and I could tell that she felt easier too after the first few moments. I asked her how her family felt about her decision and she said that they'd tried to talk her out of it, but that now they accepted it. She wanted to know what we both did for a living and she liked the answer. Each turn of the conversation flowed like a river. Later she said that she'd prepared a long list of questions to ask (so had we), but that she'd forgotten about them almost immediately. She didn't seem to be surprised by her certainty that we were the right ones and we were thrilled to have found her.

That first contact with our son's birth mother felt like it was 'meant to be' from the very beginning. It was clear that she felt the connection as strongly as we did. We simply had no doubts and neither did she. The next day, I went out and bought the first tiny little sweater for our son. I told my husband that I felt like I had leaped off a cliff; I was flying! This had all happened so quickly after making the decision to adopt a child that sometimes we felt like pinching each other to make sure we weren't dreaming. At one point, my husband said quizzically, "Isn't step one supposed to happen before step seven?" Things were moving beyond the speed of light and it was real; miraculous and real.

We had only told our families and a very few close friends that we wanted to adopt a child and here we were, a very short two weeks later, hanging up the phone from our first contact with the young woman who was going to give birth to him exactly three months from now. Our heads were spinning; we felt like we'd been shot out of some cosmic cannon. All of our molecules were rearranged, but our spirits recognized the truth and reality of what was unfolding. The 'baby soul' I'd been talking to on my daily walks for over a year-and-a-half now had found a way to come to us and it wasn't going to be through our bodies, but through this young woman's. The Law of Attraction always figures out the 'how' way better than we could!

That telephone meeting marked the beginning of an emotional and spiritual adventure that felt like a quantum leap for me and my husband and to tell you the truth, we spent the next several years learning just what it was we did and how we did it that invited such dramatic and immediate results. We're so grateful for the meta-physical teachings which have shed light on our Law of Attraction process before we even knew to call it that! The simple fact of finding each other so effortlessly thrilled through us and through everyone we shared the story with; goose bumps all around! Although we both experienced the usual uncertainties and insecu-rities in other areas of our lives; in this situation we felt no fear and no insecurity, only the deepest trust we'd ever known. We knew we were way beyond reason or rational thought in this trust. That fact was reflected frequently by many others who reminded us of every heartbreaking story they'd ever heard about adoptions that had 'fallen through.' We realized that they were only trying to protect us from enormous disappointment, but we didn't feel afraid of anything. It wasn't that we were holding the fear of this young birth mother changing her mind at bay; we simply had a knowing deeper than the ocean that she wouldn't. Our feelings about the rightness of this were huge and we had a hard time convincing others that they didn't need to worry either. Our baby was on his way!

I had begun to experience my love for this child the moment I began talking to his 'baby soul' eighteen months earlier as I walked in the park near our home, along the canal, under the huge blue sky. At that time, I held in very open hands the possibility of him coming to us. I'd say, "We're here, waiting for you if you want and need us to be your mommy and daddy. But, if that's not what you need right now; it's okay. We love you forever." I surprised myself with the unselfish nature of my thoughts. I knew that I could be quite the opposite when I really wanted something. But this was different. A part of me seemed to know that it wasn't just about MY plan to have a child with my beloved husband. What this child's soul was planning for himself held a higher value for me. It could be no other way for me.

Now please understand, this approach was something I

struggled with a lot in other areas of my life, but in this situation, all the grasping, fear and desire to control had fallen away. I was in a state of grace. I was really okay with either outcome; baby or no baby. But it now seemed clear; the baby was coming!

So once this was apparent, the universe decided to get playful. For example, I looked at the antique green rocker in the nursery and thought, "Gosh, it's so….green. Hmmmm…" Literally, the next moment the doorbell rang and when I opened the door, the woman standing there, a client of mine, said, "Please show me the nursery." I took her to the baby's room where she opened a bag she was carrying, took out a quilt she had just finished making and flung it over the rocker, saying emphatically, "There!"…and covering that old rocker beautifully. For the next three months, it was like the old saying, "from my lips to God's ears" which is a poetic way of expressing how Law of Attraction operates. Whatever desire I expressed; bingo! An immediate manifestation took place. We were in a state of constant, grateful awe and we knew that our entire beings were being re-calibrated or something; we knew this was how life was supposed to be!

Something else started happening, too. Frequently, I would respond to something I thought my husband had said and he'd look at me like I had just sprouted wings and exclaim, "But I didn't say that, I was only thinking it." At one point, we looked at each other and said, "You know, if by some crazy twist of fate, this baby doesn't come, he has already shaken up our reality, deepened our spirituality and has us swimming in an ocean of love; he's taught us how life is supposed to be lived and has already changed us forever."

Three months to the day of the first contact with my son's birth mother, we brought him home from the hospital at the tender age of 24 hours. Seventeen years later, he is still shaking up our reality, deepening our spirituality, swimming with us in an ocean of love and teaching us how life is supposed to be lived; changing us forever. Now we know that what occurred is the Law of Attraction; when we're not calling it a miracle!

—Janice Masters
www.EverydayJoy.com

Find Your Passion

In the summer of 2004, I began reevaluating my life; I really didn't like the direction I was headed. I was the Payroll Manager for my father's company in the automotive industry and I was soon to be promoted to Human Resources & Payroll Manager. I was thrilled at the idea of having been entrusted with so much responsibility, but I was also a little petrified at the same time. Something wasn't right; something was missing.

I worked very hard to learn absolutely everything I could about my duties. I went to conferences with the hope that there was some missing link that would tie everything together and I would finally have the job that I'd always wanted. That missing link never showed its face, so I began searching for a way out.

I knew in my heart that there had to be something out there for me that was rewarding both spiritually and financially. For example, I love working with animals but can't see them suffer, so being a vet was out. Volunteering at the Humane Society was wonderful, but I could never earn a living that way. There had to be something out there for me. I just knew it.

I had never heard of the Law of Attraction at this point in my life. I grew up with a father that strictly emphasized the need to work very hard in order to succeed in life. Money didn't grow on trees. Even throughout school, my successful efforts were rarely praised; especially if he could find something negative to comment on, elsewhere. Nothing was ever good enough and I always had to work harder. Many of us have been through this very situation, so I know I'm not alone. The Law of Attraction would have been a joke to him. As I got older, I began to question his theory that conforming and working hard was the only way. To me, it just didn't make sense. Why would people make themselves unhappy on purpose?

My Human Resources position didn't please me and I began doing just the bare minimum in my job. That was obviously unrewarding and I had to make a change. But how could I do that?

Two years after I began my search for 'something else', I found a business opportunity that seemed way too good to be true. The basis was teaching the Law of Attraction to others and helping them through what I went through. It was the best thing that had ever happened to me. They introduced me to the movie, *The Secret*, and I knew I had found what I was looking for. I have a passion for helping others and this allowed me to do that and support myself financially at the same time. How was this possible? How had I found the two separate things I was looking for, in one neat little package?

The answer is the Law of Attraction. I thought that this business had randomly found me. However, I began to realize that I, in fact, had drawn this business to me. I wanted freedom, spiritually, emotionally and financially and I was putting out to the universe all the details and I got it! I am stress free and I no longer have any worries. All of my friends, even my family members, have seen my transformation and they now respond to me with the utmost respect. I followed my passion, despite all the negativity I received and am now living my dream. All thanks to the Law of Attraction. It is more powerful than I could have ever imagined.

—Tina Block
www.NohonaEnterprises.com

Nothin' but Net

I have experienced many Law of Attraction 'events.' Before I'd ever heard of the LOA, I chose to attract a job in the IT field; I was changing careers and decided that I wouldn't settle for less and went on to describe the job in detail. What I would do, how I felt and how much the salary would be, the hours, my office and other details were all mapped out in my head. I had my resume on *Monster.com* and focused on these details and feelings and it felt real; like it was happening right now. I let it go like a balloon and felt my stress, tension and anxiety about finding a job release.

This was on a Thursday and on the following Monday, I got an email from a recruiter who had found my resume on *Monster.com* and thought I would be a perfect fit for a small company that needed my exact skill set and had a budget to match my salary requirements. He knew the owners of the company and as a personal favor to them he was helping them find the right person for the position. BAM ! They interviewed me and I was hired within the week. Talk about a quick manifestation!

About six weeks ago, I moved from Long Beach, California to Vancouver, Washington; I was short on cash but 'knew' I should relocate. Take the leap and a net will appear. Anyway, I did everything; got a place to live and sold a lot of stuff to raise cash for gas money. On the day that I was driving to Vancouver, after I'd sold most everything and had enough cash to buy gas for the trip, but not enough to pay the rent, I was on an errand and out of the blue, a guy pulls out in front of me and I couldn't avoid hitting his vehicle. I freaked out, since I was supposed to drive out of state within hours and my signal light was broken. Who knows where else there was damage to my car? But the guy said he was sorry; it was totally his fault. He felt bad, but he didn't want to turn it in to insurance so he said, "I'll give you $2,000 cash and you can get it fixed later."

I called my mechanic, who quizzed me about the damage and told me to take the cash and stop by so he could wire up my light. My mechanic checked out my car for structural safety, wired up the light and I went on my way with only a little cosmetic damage to my car. Wow! Talk about a net appearing! I now had the cash to make the rent and living expenses while I found a job in my new location. If one were to try to imagine this scenario; I just don't see how anyone could imagine this series of events.

I have found over the years that I've been practicing and using the Law of Attraction without knowing what it was or that it had a name. I read Lynn Grabhorn's book, *Excuse Me, Your Life is Waiting*, a few years ago and realized that I have been doing this for quite some time; without realizing that I was using it to attract some things that I didn't want.

When I saw *The Secret*, I realized just how powerful I really was and that the more one practices and uses the principles, the more adept one gets. I believe we will eventually be able to manifest whatever we want!

—Jeannine Shingler
www.freshroots.net

Change of Heart

I had been a US Peace Corps trainee in Ethiopia, East Africa the year before. But I had terminated and gone home just three weeks into training for personal reasons. By 1974, I was trying to get back with the Peace Corps in Ethiopia and was being helped a lot by Ed Marcus, the Desk Officer for Peace Corps, Ethiopia in Washington, DC.

Ed had given me three other country options, but he was adamant that I couldn't return to Ethiopia; or any other country in Africa. I had decided to go to the Philippines when I received an interesting call from Ed. He told me that the Director of PC, Ethiopia, Dr. Jack Mills, had come to Washington for a meeting the next day. He would be returning to Ethiopia that same evening. Ed said that if I really wanted to return to Ethiopia, I had to get myself up to Washington (from Florida). He said he might be able to get me in to see Dr. Mills for a few minutes; but there would be no guarantees.

I hopped on the earliest plane and landed in Washington at about 6pm; too late to get in to see Dr. Mills that evening. So, I roamed around Washington and I wound up on a park bench between the Lincoln Memorial and the Washington Monument. I was just sitting there, scratching my head. I knew just what I wanted; to go back to Ethiopia. But I had no idea what I was going to say to Dr. Mills. How would I convince this man to let me go back and teach in Ethiopia?

Then one word entered my head. There among the ghosts of our forefathers, this one word began to pound and pound in my brain! It was the Law of Attraction at work. It was providing me with the one thing that I could say to Dr. Mills that had any chance of convincing him. That one word, yelling in my mind, was the word, Truth.

Tell him the truth; that's all I had to do. In my mind, I could picture Dr. Mills and myself alone in his office the next day. I could actually hear him ask me why I had left the previous year. What on Earth were the personal reasons that had kept me from staying in Ethiopia? There was no mistaking the absolute certainty I felt. I knew beyond any shadow of doubt that I would convince Jack

Mills and return to Ethiopia! In a fraction of a second I had gone from confused and worried to certain and confident.

The next morning found me in the Peace Corps office, sitting next to Ed Marcus' desk. Dr. Mills was still in his meeting, so I waited for him. All of a sudden, Dr. Mills came crashing through the door and disappeared into his private office. It was evident that things hadn't gone well at his meeting. Ed gave me a glance that pretty much said, 'Sorry I wasted your time.' He went into Dr. Mills' office to ask if I could see him for a few minutes. When he walked back out, he told me, "Dr. Mills will give you five minutes and not a moment more."

I walked into Dr. Mills' office and sat down. His first question was the one I had anticipated. So I told him the truth about why I had left Ethiopia the previous year. It took twenty minutes, but Dr. Mills kept listening. When I finished, he said, "If I let you go back to Ethiopia, you have to promise me that you'll not terminate early. I have to know that you will stick to your commitment." So I promised him and he said I could return to Ethiopia!

After twenty minutes, I walked out of the office and told Ed Marcus. Ed exclaimed, "No way! He just told me that there was no way he would let you go back; no way!" I just beamed and said, "Go ask him yourself, if you don't believe me." Ed actually did this and when he came back, shaking his head in disbelief, he explained it to me. "Do you know why Jack Mills is here?" I shook my head. "He's here for the express purpose of getting the Peace Corps pulled out of Ethiopia! Haile Selassie has been arrested and jailed and there's so much violence! Jack's worried that all of his volunteers and staff will get hurt. But in the meeting, his bosses turned him down. It's just unbelievable that after all that, he's going to let you go back to Ethiopia; unbelievable!"

I had convinced a man who had a reputation for never changing his mind; for being intractable. All I did was to give him what the Law of Attraction had given me; all I did was tell him the truth. There were so many things about the situation that I had had no control over.

Yet, where I left off and could do no more, the Law of Attraction took over and turned the impossible around. I didn't just lie around waiting for things to happen; that's not how the Law of

Attraction works. You do all that you can do and the Law of Attraction does the rest!

—Scott Ley
http://eBook-eDen.Secretsgolden.com

Meeting My Soul Mate

I already had proof that miracles exist and that the Law of Attraction works. I had been using it for years to manifest great friends, homes and a successful career. In 1997, I decided to apply these techniques to manifest my soul mate. I had spent the previous year forgiving myself and others for relationships that didn't work out, I had made a list of what I wanted in a man and released it to the universe and I had unhooked myself energetically from past lovers; I truly believed in my heart that my soul mate was out there. Now I was hoping for a little cosmic power boost to bring us together.

On June 22, 1997, I went to see Amma, the hugging saint from India. I had heard about her years earlier from Deepak Chopra, who said to me, "Amma's the real thing. If you ever have a chance to get a hug from her, do it." I signed up to attend a weekend retreat, knowing that during this retreat I would receive at least two hugs. On the first evening of the retreat, I patiently waited in line for my hug. I was excited and a little nervous; I had a plan, but I didn't know if it would work. I had been told that Amma doesn't speak English and that when you receive a hug, she may whisper or chant into your ear; but you mustn't converse with her. When it was my turn and while she was hugging me, I whispered in her ear, "Dear Amma, please heal my heart of anything that is stopping me from finding my soul mate." She laughed as I said this and squeezed me tighter and I knew that she had understood my prayer.

That night, I had a very vivid dream. In the dream, there were seven women, dressed in purple, singing to me. The lyrics of the song were, "Arielle is the woman that comes after Beth." When I woke up in the morning, I was convinced it had been a sign; my soul mate was out there, but he was currently with someone named Beth. The next evening, I had an opportunity for a second hug from Amma. This time, I whispered in her ear to please send me my soul mate and I rattled off part of my wish list. Again, she laughed and squeezed me tight. Three weeks later, I went on an unexpected business trip to Portland, Oregon and Brian, my client's business partner, met me at the airport. The moment I saw him, I had the thought, "I wonder who Beth is?"

Now, I am not one to hear voices and I never had before, but later that day I very clearly heard a voice say to me, "He's the one. This is how it happens. This is who you are going to spend your life with."

Soon after that, Brian turned to me and said, "When I picked you up at the airport, did I look familiar to you?" I said, "Yes, why do you ask?" He said, "Because I've been dreaming about you." By the end of the day, I found out that he'd been seeing me in his dreams and had recently ended a relationship with a woman named Elizabeth!

Brian and I became engaged three weeks later. Within two months, he had moved to La Jolla to live with me. Exactly one year to the date that I asked Amma to help me find my soul mate, she married us in a Hindu ceremony in front of thousands of people.

Miracles do come true and the Law of Attraction totally works.

—Arielle Ford
www.soulmatekit.com

We Create with our Mind

I like the idea of creating jewelry with positive affirmations and healing messages because you could keep it on your person, no matter where you were or what you were doing. After reading *Zero Limits*, I began to draw and design different styles of jewelry with the four phrases, "I'm sorry, please forgive me, I love you, thank you" and pictured them being made out of sterling silver and 14K gold. I noticed that the moment I started to create, I became more peaceful, happy and fulfilled. I would go into a peaceful trance and there I could access everything I needed. I didn't have a clue where I was going to go in order to have all of my designs made, but I knew that the universe didn't need me micro-managing its job. It takes care of the *how*, while we take care of the *what*. When we work

with the Law of Attraction, a
necessary ingredient is to trust.
So, once I finished with my
what, I gave the rest over to the
universe;, trusting that it would
take my ideas and do something
even better with them.

The following week, I
received an email from a jeweler
who had questions about *Zero
Limits* and she wrote, "Also, I have a gift I would like to send to Joe.
I'm still working on it, but it will be done within the next couple of
weeks; do you know where I should send it?"

When I asked to see her finished artistry, I couldn't help but
smile; I recognized her gifts as the very same drawings I had created
by hand just a week before. We are a perfect example of the Law of
Attraction at work as defined by *physics*: "The Law of Attraction *is*
the electric or magnetic force that acts between oppositely charged
bodies, tending to draw them together."

Not only did she create the exact pieces I had designed and
drawn by hand, but she also brought a level of topnotch skill and
expertise to the products and expanded the line in ways that I
hadn't even imagined. This is where the 'or better' part comes into
play; that's how the Law of Attraction works. When we live in the
flow, our experiences can be so easy, clear and even; miraculous!

—Suzanne Burns
www.IntentionalTreasures.com

Payson's perspective

My name is Payson Cooper and I'm a jewelry designer and creator.
I read *Zero Limits* last year and absolutely loved it. I was inspired
while reading it and while listening to the first workshop recording
with Dr. Hew Len and Joe [Vitale] to create a jewelry line using the
Ho'oponopono clearing phrases, "I love you. I'm sorry. Please forgive me. Thank you." I created the jewelry line; two styles of rings
and two styles of necklaces. One style I began to picture immedi-

ately as I was reading the book; the spiral. Since, as Joe says, "Money likes speed." I immediately sent several of each item to Joe and Dr. Hew Len to thank them for the book and the amazing impact it's having on my life.

In order to get a mailing address for Joe, I emailed the contact information on his website and heard back from Suzanne Burns, Joe's lovely and wonderful assistant. When I shared with her that I was interested in sending Joe something I made, inspired by Ho'oponopono she sent me to her website to see some of the items she offers. We became fast friends through email and in a short time, she became the exclusive retailer for the Payson & Co., LLC Ho'oponopono Jewelry Line! Suzanne has become a wonderful friend, as well as client, creating other jewelry pieces with me for her business as well.

I am truly honored and blessed to have received the inspiration for the Ho'oponopono designs and for the actions, which seemed so simple and which have led directly to an amazing and wonderful new friend, as well as an incredible business contact.

—Payson Cooper
http://www.transformationaljewelry.com

Sweet Deal

I've always owned other people's vehicles. My credit is awful, but I couldn't stop picturing myself driving all over the Eastern US in a new car. After I read Joe [Vitale]'s email, I decided to go to a Kia dealership, but my car turned into the Hyundai lot instead. The salesman offered me a 2008 Hyundai Elantra with all the bells and whistles I wanted; pending approval of financing. My ambition was to get a car with no money down, XM satellite radio installed in it and monthly payments under $400. I test drove one I liked and then went home. I called the sales rep the next day, but he was too busy with a customer to give me any feedback. By Monday, my frustrations grew and I decided to go to the Honda and Nissan dealerships in my town. The Honda salesman wanted to lease me a car that didn't ring my chimes. It had none of my bells and whistles, plus he required $1,111 down; monthly payments would be $425. The Nissan guy asked for a $200 check to have a vehicle delivered that he would hold for me. He said he would be away until Wednesday and would call me when he got back.

On Wednesday, the Hyundai salesman called and asked me to come and pick up my new car. After crying on Tuesday and part of Wednesday morning, wondering if I'd get out of my old car, this was welcome news. Shortly afterward, the Nissan guy called and said he would need $5,000 to clear my negative equity on my trade-in car. I told him I didn't have that kind of money and I would stop by later to get my check back. Imagine the surprised look on the Nissan salesman's face when I drove up from the Hyundai dealership two doors down in my new 2008 Hyundai Elantra, with all the bells and whistles!

—*My Way AND the Highway*
by Evelyn Hargrove

CHAPTER 8

Igniting the Divine Within

It is a curious challenge to explain how awareness evolves in the life of every person. First, you must realize that you don't know what you don't know. Your results are a product of what you have been taught and learned over your life, not because you consciously chose your beliefs. Once you recognize that your beliefs may be irrational or self-limiting, you can consciously choose to change. This is done by clearing those negative thoughts and beliefs and replacing them with positive ones.

We are human and in our present existence, we don't normally move off our duffs unless we're forced to. Many of us rattle along life's highway with our same old thought process; not really doing bad, but not reaching our full potential. A few people experience what is known as a catalyst of awareness. This could be through dissatisfaction with life or a traumatic event that forces them to view their current beliefs from a new perspective and evaluate whether those beliefs serve their purpose. This empowers you to take control and choose to attract what you want in life.

The last stage of awareness is the understanding that you must let go. You must release your desire and allow the miracles to come to you. This may seem a little counterintuitive, since I just said that you must be aware to take control and choose. However, remember that I said awareness is about enhancing and pumping up the power associated with the Law of Attraction? This last step gives you the maximum power to attract things into your life. By letting go of the intention, you allow yourself to co-create with the divine and deliver your heart's desire in the easiest and fastest way possible. If you hold on to the 'how', you will struggle more than is necessary. Letting go makes it easier.

Everyone has a different idea of what the divine is; some say God, Universe, Buddha or any number of labels. In essence, they're all the same. As you focus your intentions on helping others, you're naturally rewarded with your desires. You move from Ego Intentions to Divine Intentions and divine intentions are the ones that attract the fastest.

Letting go isn't about tossing your intentions to the wind. It's about focusing your intent and then releasing the 'how.' This allows the universe to do its work without interference from you. Quite honestly, most people put more obstacles in their way than is necessary because they don't really trust the divine to deliver; they have to interfere and dictate how things should happen.

You are the one with the power to create whatever it is you want in life, so it all starts with your intentions. If your life sucks, it's because you created it that way. If your life is awesome, it's because you made it that way. The key to success is working backward. First, discover your life purpose, your calling, your gifts and your strengths, then proceed to do your work. Most people work hoping they can find their life purpose. Before they know it, life has passed them by. The key then, to letting go is to first know what your life purpose is. Then letting go takes on a new look. It's letting go with a purpose rather than letting go and wishing for the best.

When faced with difficult decisions, you always have a choice and indecision or doing nothing is one of those choices. Don't sit back and just hope that the Law of Attraction is going to support you. The Law of Attraction always delivers, even if it's not something you want. You are responsible for your own choices. While that may give some people a sinking feeling, you can choose to revel in the fact that the power is in your hands to change whatever isn't working for you.

Some of the best miracles happen when you've already released the intention and then it suddenly arrives out of the blue and shocks you with how perfect a solution it provides. Chris' story is a great example.

I do Prosperity Consciousness talks. I was diversifying into Real Estate when I got an email invitation from Nan, an officer of the *Real Estate Club*. She was speaking about an investment tour at a restaurant. My dad and I decided to go. I happened to sit right next to Nan. We were the last to leave, as we were having a long, interesting conversation. We had a lot in common. Over the next two months, we met for lunch and ran into each other often. We spoke about business, real estate and international investments. One night, I attended a meditation class. As I was leaving the room, I ran right into her! It was strange. We wandered the store, talking about spirituality, law of attraction and so on. We kept running into each other all over town in unrelated places. I was single, but wasn't really looking for a relationship, so at first I didn't notice all these 'coincidences.'

Nan invited me to her Women's Real Estate group to give my Prosperity Consciousness talk. It was the best talk I've given and the conversation included suggesting books. Both Nan and I recommended *The Attractor Factor* by Joe Vitale; one more thing in common! After a long, lively evening, everyone left. We talked until one in the morning in the parking lot! We just kept finding more interesting things to talk about like religion, spirituality and the universe. I had a lovely time.

Then I received an email from Joe Vitale about a dinner with Dr. Hew Len, who cured a whole building of mentally ill people without talking to them. I had to see this. I invited the only person that I thought would appreciate it; Nan. We drove together and talked a lot. The dinner and talk were wonderful. The energy was expanding and filled with possibilities. We were enjoying each other's company so much that we continued talking in the lobby bar; having a wonderful time. Mind you, I was still thinking that I wasn't looking for a relationship!

Over the next four hours, my life changed forever. The conversation got more and more interesting. Then, in one instant, I got the clear realization that she was the best candidate for dating I'd seen in over a decade. I told her I was interested in her on the spot. Funny thing was; she'd been feeling the same way for weeks. We had gone to a jazz club with a friend the week before and she was trying to see if the energy was coming from me; but I hadn't noticed. At the New Age bookstore, she got a little scared because she could feel my energy before I came out of the meditation class. She was wondering why she felt such strong energy when around me.

Well, once I felt it, we both fell madly in love. We've been together for over two years and are happier than ever. The honeymoon doesn't have to end! Neither of us had been actively looking for a relationship. We were pursuing our own happiness and creating abundant lives. We expected life to be good. Our energies match because we both believe the purpose of life is to be happy. We expect miracles and let the universe figure out all the details. Take your next action step and continue to move forward. Then, be aware of who and what is showing up over and over again around you!

—Chris Sherrod
AbundanceUnlimited.com

We all have inspiration; thoughts and ideas of what our life could be. Yet, some people just don't recognize it. When we release the 'how', we're open to receiving miracles and expect them. All kinds of things can begin to happen. The synchronicity in our lives occurs more often; events coincide with other events and you begin to see the flow of the divine through your life, like a river.

Inspiration originates with the Divine and if you act on that inspiration and then release it back to the divine, you reap the rewards. It may come as a soft whisper of inspiration or a sudden explosion of excited thought; both are capable of giving you what you want most out of life, even if you're not sure how it will happen. Say you have a desire for greater wealth in your life and you also have a hobby you're passionate about. So you align yourself with source and then a little thought trickles in, '*what if* I do this and this and this with my hobby and turn it into a business?' So you research it (action), you develop a business plan (action) and you find your market; you build your store (online or otherwise) or consign your product for sale. Wow! Money starts coming in.

Inspired action is following each step as it appears before you. Like Dr. Martin Luther King said, "You don't have to see the whole staircase; you just have to take the *first step*."

Committing to inspired action is a step-by-step process. You have to take it one step at a time. You don't have to see the whole picture. Go with the piece you have in hand. Do what your heart says to do. On the long road, you can't go wrong.

You can accomplish anything by taking one step at a time. It is the same with the creation of the life you want to live. If you try and look at the whole project or the big picture of what you want to do in your life it will scare you. Most walk away and don't even try. The trick is to focus on the moment, focus and do what is asked of you in the moment, for that is truly *your only place of power*.

Craig and I had been renting a barn/apartment on a 92-acre farm in Fauquier County, Virginia. We'd started running a lovely herd of Black Angus beef cattle which helped offset the cost of living outside Washington, DC. We'd formed Hideout Horse and Cattle Co. in 2005 to take advantage of the agriculture tax exemptions. The farm hadn't been officially named by the landlord, but as it nestled against Rattlesnake Mountain in the foothills of the Blue Ridge Mountains, I began calling it "The Hideout". It also fit Craig's attitude; he's terribly sorry he never got to be a real outlaw and with the number of horses, cats, dogs, and cows we had, we were quite a gang! The concept of the Hideout just grew from there.

I had a good job with a 'start-up' IT consulting firm and Craig had a good job in the construction division of a local landscaping/nursery firm. As we thought more and more about buying property in the southwest and realizing our dream of developing a guest ranch, the more I realized I would have to switch jobs and Craig would have to be full-time on the ranch. The challenge was to continue earning the high salary I was making so we could make our dream a reality. In the form of a lovely friend, that very avenue opened up to me. She was also a Production 'Guru' who worked as a consultant; traveling the country producing Government proposals and related products and she made great money. We struck up a friendship and she recommended me to her company. The beauty of this job switch was I could live anywhere I wanted; including the middle of the High Desert southwest and still work in the corporate world, making very good money. The only drawback was that I would have to travel and be away from home for weeks or months at a time.

I made the switch and was rewarded with a good hourly rate and high praise from the two weeks of intensive training. Immediately upon 'graduation,' I was assigned to an account fairly local to the farm. I was away from home during the week, but was able to go home every weekend. In the meantime, Craig had gone to Arizona and purchased Hideout Ranch. My 401K from my previous company paid the down payment and we had until January before the first note was due. So, I worked for two months solid, got in lots of hours, got some great experience and really made some good impressions. Then, the assignment I thought I would be deployed upon didn't pan out and I went home to wait on the next one. That was the *other* drawback; if I don't work, I don't get paid. So, the first week of January, I was home. I was home until the end of January, creeping into February. We had our first ranch note due in January, we were about to move eight horses, a dog, twelve cats and however many bovines we decided to take and I was sitting at home, not earning a thing.

Then, on a Thursday night, my cell phone rang which was odd because suddenly we were getting cell signals in the kitchen! Anyway, I was thrilled to see it was from a friend whom I had determined to be a true kindred spirit. Imagine my surprise when she said, "There's someone who wants to talk to you," and the next voice I heard was *Dr. Joe Vitale*! We had a fabulous conversation and I told him how worried I was about not working and all the expenses we were facing. That's when he told me about writing essentially a 'Thank you note' for what it was I wanted. I remember him saying I needed to be specific in what I was being grateful for and almost effusive in my thanks. So, when Craig went down to start the grill for dinner, I sat down immediately and followed Dr. Vitale's suggestion exactly and I felt better for doing so!

The next morning, the phone rang. It was headquarters, telling me to call a fellow Production Associate I'd worked with before and to report on Monday. I wasn't really surprised I'd gotten a call; just thrilled. I thanked Dr. Vitale out loud. I've been working steadily ever since; except for the week I needed time off to move. As luck would have it, I'm headed home for what I think is just a couple or three days, but it may stretch out to a week. I'm not worried about my next assignment. I know exactly how to make it happen.

—Tamara J. Lawson
www.hideoutranch.com

Trust

'Let Go and Trust' is something you hear a lot if you hang around self-development gurus for even a short period of time. Sometimes, it seems like the best answer to questions we think up about how something's going to manifest or why something seems to be taking so long to come into form. After a while, it can also seem like the answer we give when we really have no answer to give.

It's important to know that this is an integral part of your understanding, but just one step in the journey. Usually, it's the best thing to do when we want to release 'manual' control or forceful manipulation of physical reality; which is based on fear of change. This step is about opening up to an expanded sense of self. When we try to control something, we're limiting our 'creation' to that which we've already done; we're limiting ourselves to what we already know. Most of the time, we're afraid that if we release control, things will lead to disaster faster than you can say, "Let go and trust."

In learning to trust our own creative, spontaneous energy, we have to learn to open to the unknown; to what wants to be born, like an artist at an easel. For instance, if all you know is lack or negative events, then you'll need to open yourself to another option in order to create something different. But, accepting the vulnerability of not knowing for awhile, without closing down and going back to what's familiar, takes a certain amount of strength and determination and maybe even practice. That's what the whole idea of trust is about and why you hear it so often.

Matt's story is a great example of letting go and allowing good things to flow through your life.

I have experienced the Law of Attraction in numerous areas of my life so far. Some of the time, I didn't even realize it was at work until I looked back and thought about the situations I was in. Unfortunately, some of them were what we call 'negative' experiences, although now I think that they were all positive and useful for the feedback they provided.

I was born with a condition called Erbs Palsy, which meant my nerves were torn from my spine and my left arm was left paralyzed. As I grew, doctors told my parents and me that I wouldn't be able to play any sport, swim or play any musical instruments. This was the image that they had in their head and what they had seen in others. However, the image I had for my life differed from my parents'.

I began swimming lessons, though I found it hard at first. I used to swim in circles because my right arm was a lot stronger than my left. I set my mind on swimming a whole length of the pool and one day I finally managed to do it. I also developed a passion for cricket at a young age. I wanted to play cricket for my county, I also wanted to be captain for my local village team. I focused and visualized with all my might. Eventually, my coach put me in for county trials and I made it onto the squad. I played Semi Professional cricket for five years. I captained my university team and now, my local village team. I know that anything is possible if you put your mind to it. It only needs passion and emotion.

In the past, I've had negative experiences with bullying at school. At the time, I was focusing on the name calling and nasty actions that other children would engage in. I now realize that my focus was attracting more of what I didn't want. It wasn't until one day that I just ignored them that it started to disappear and I became one of the popular kids at school. I also attracted exam results. I remember a month before my exams, I wrote down the grades that I wanted to receive. I asked the universe and let it go. The results day arrived and to my amazement, my grades were exactly the same as the ones I had written down, prior to the test.

I studied fine art in university and my focus was on my frustration with the world. I was painting subjects of war and terrorism. I wanted to make people aware that we need to make changes in the world. The problem was that it was dragging me down emotionally. My grades started to slip and I became very angry. I lived in a house with eight other people. I was suffering from sleepless nights. Two of my housemates were listening to very negative music and played it late at night and very loud. I was so depressed and I didn't know why. One day, I was looking at images of George Bush on the internet. I decided to paint this image in a cartoon fashion surrounded by fluffy clouds. My tutors hated it, but everyone else loved it. This was a turning point for me, as I realized that it was my perception and how I viewed things in my life that created my attitude and attracted my results.

I was approaching my subjects in a more comical way and my whole life changed. You see, when you focus on things with a passion it can affect your whole life. I had a call one day from a gallery; they wanted me to show my art work in an exhibition. I was attracting them because I had changed my thoughts and actions. I sold a painting before the exhibition had even opened and then went on to sell three more in the same month! I then attracted one of my dream cars a few months later and a holiday to New York for me, my girlfriend and my parents.

I'd been told all my life that I would never play any musical instruments. But one day, I felt inspired to pick up a guitar. I naturally picked it up the wrong way round. I was playing left handed. I can't turn my arm over to play chords, but I can finger pick and strum. My parents bought me a left handed guitar for one of my birthdays. While I was in university, I started to develop my songwriting skills and recorded a demo album with a friend of mine who had a small recording studio. I started to really enjoy music and for the last two years, I've been writing and recording an album that I've poured my heart and soul into. My roommate works as a professional musician and his boss is a phenomenal musician and has worked with some amazing people. One day, I asked the universe for him to work with me on my new album. I came home one night and I spoke to my roommate. He said that he had played a couple of my songs for his boss and he thought that they were great. He offered to conduct a full string section and orchestrate the album. I couldn't believe it! I then remembered that a few days before, I had also asked the universe for a full orchestra to play on my album. For my first album, we had used sampled strings and I wanted to use real strings for the passion and the quality of sound. We're due to record in the coming months and everything that I asked for is coming into place. I took Joe Vitale's advice by taking 'inspired action.' I recently had an urge to start writing. A few weeks later I had a book that was all about my feelings, experiences and my thoughts about the world, spirituality and my experiences with the Law of Attraction. I asked for a self publishing company to appear for me. I came across the perfect one and now have a book! I thank Joe for his book, *The Key*; it truly inspired me.

—Matt Parsons
www.mattparsonsartandmusic.com

Matt shows what can happen if you let go and trust. He had more obstacles than most to overcome, yet he wasn't concerned with all the things that others thought he couldn't do. He set his intention, took inspired action and let go.

Often, a person's resistance to the idea of letting go and trusting is really them refusing to let go. They are trying too hard and keep beating their heads against brick walls, running into obstacle after obstacle. If you trust your inspiration when it tells you to do something and let go of the need for control, the path becomes clear. Trust the divine within you and follow that inner guidance. When you stop insisting on knowing so much about every situation, you allow yourself to accept and learn and you will find a better and easier way.

It is very much like standing in a stream. If you insist on knowing where the next firm step is, it's very much like walking upstream. However, if you let go and allow the stream to do the work for you, life is much easier. The Law of Attraction is the current and can carry you beyond all you have imagined. But, it will only work if you let go and allow it to do so. You must stop the habit of worrying and stressing over the details, as that is proof that you haven't let go of your need for control.

This can take some practice. You may not believe it, but for most of the first part of my life, I was an introvert. I could never have imagined being in front of a group of people and speaking; let alone appearing in movies or videos. Now, I can't imagine not doing those things. Once I let go of the fear and need to control every aspect of my life, it improved tremendously! I always get a chuckle out of those people who are shocked at how much better their lives become when they get out of the way! Stop trying to manage the little stuff and allow the divine to bring miracles into your life, every day.

Once you firmly grasp the idea that miracles are possible in your life every day, it becomes easy to expect. Still, I'm often surprised when they show up! This is probably because I notice them more now, as my mind isn't so cluttered with all the details that I used to want to control. I now release those and it allows room for me to accept the gifts that are waiting for my life. You can be a part of this, too. In fact, you already are. You are standing in the stream as we speak, but you're either walking against the current or letting it carry you along. The question is, are you ready to let go?

Your Challenge

Now that you've come to the end of the book, what are you going to do with what you've learned?

You have choices, of course. You can do nothing. You can re-read this book. You can buy copies for family and friends. You can encourage others to read this book by writing reviews, blog posts and more.

But I want to challenge you. I want you to think bigger than you've ever thought before. I want you to *dare something worthy*.

After all, if you could have, do, or be anything, what would you want?

If you knew you wouldn't fail, what would you do?

If you won millions of dollars in the lottery and all your bills were paid and your future was secure, what would you do then?

Whatever your answer is; go do it now.

Dare Something Worthy.

About the Author

One of the stars of the movies *The Secret, The Opus, The Compass* and *Try It On Everything,* Dr. Joe Vitale is President of Hypnotic Marketing, Inc. and President of Frontier Nutritional Research, Inc., both companies based outside of Austin, Texas.

He is the author of way too many books to list here, including the #1 best-selling book *The Attractor Factor,* the #1 best-seller *Life's Missing Instruction Manual* and the best-selling Nightingale-Conant audioprogram, *The Power of Outrageous Marketing* as well as the two new programs, *The Missing Secret* and *The Awakening Course.*

He's also written *The Key, Zero Limits, The E-Code, Meet and Grow Rich, There's A Customer Born Every Minute, The Seven Lost Secrets of Success, Hypnotic Writing, Your Internet Cash Machine, Buying Trances* and *Inspired Marketing,* all for J. Wiley.

Once homeless and living in poverty, Joe is now considered one of the pioneers of Internet marketing. He has made millionaires and helped create online empires.

Due to his work in *The Secret,* and to the success of his books, *The Attractor Factor* and *Zero Limits,* he is now becoming known as a self-help guru. He's often called the Buddha of the Internet.

His main website is at http://www.mrfire.com.